The Electric Spark that Jumps

Derek Alway

"I fly because it releases my mind from the tyranny of petty things."

- Antoine de Sainte-Exupery

"The airplane is just a bunch of sticks and wires and cloth, a tool for learning about the sky and about what kind of person I am, when I fly. An airplane stands for freedom, for joy, for the power to understand, and to demonstrate that understanding. Those things aren't destructible."

- Richard Bach

"This thing we call luck is merely professionalism and attention to detail; it's your awareness of everything that is going on around you; it's how well you know and understand your airplane and your own limitations. Luck is the sum total of your abilities as an aviator. If you think your luck is running low, you'd better get busy and make some more. Work harder. Pay more attention. Study your handbook and procedures. Do better preflights.

- Stephen Coonts
US Navy flying book

"For pilots sometimes see behind the curtain, behind the gossamer velvet, and find the truth behind man, the forces behind the universe."

— *Richard Bach*

"There is a little electric spark that jumps, someplace inside you, the moment you really understand something. It feels good. Watch for it!"

— *Wolfgang Langeweische*

"The wind and the waves are always on the side of the ablest navigators."

— *Edward Gibbon*

*To My Much Loved Children - Simon and Louise and
to shared memories of their beautiful mother, Angela.*

Contents

Bush Tucker Lunch in Western Australia 7

Canada 2009 Diary 15

The Lancaster Bomber 42

An Angel watches Over Me 55

Closing the Loop 68

The Day We Went to Bantry 127

San Luis Obispo 155

Tusen Takk 173

Naked Virgins Dancing on the Village Green 197

Bush Tucker Lunch in Western Australia

"Shall we go mud crabbing?" asked Lou.

"Sure," I replied, with no idea what to expect. I vaguely thought it would be a bit like looking for cockles on the mudflats at Weston-super-Mare after the tide had gone out.

The holiday was my birthday present to my daughter. Bonding time. We had driven 200 kilometres north from Broome in our four wheel drive Nissan Patrol, to Cape

Leveque. We were at the tip of the Dampier Peninsula, with King Sound on one side and the Indian Ocean to the west. The peninsula's name originates from the English explorer and buccaneer William Dampier, who in 1688 sailed his ship, the Cygnet, to New Holland (as Australia was then named) and first set foot on the peninsula. In 1803 it was again visited, this time by the French three-masted frigate, Geographe, under the command of Capitaine Nicolas Baudin. He named the cape after the ship's hydrographer, Pierre Leveque.

We had booked two nights in Kooljaman, an Aboriginal wilderness camp owned by the Bardi people of the Djarindjin and One Arm Point communities. The journey, from the pearl farming town of Broome, had begun on tarmac roads but after twenty kilometres it became a red dirt track, which continued for much of the way. The colours were spectacular. The deep rich orangey red earth road was bordered by bright green shrubs and eucalyptus trees with their ghostly white barks, all this under the canopy of a cloudless bright blue sky.

Lou drove the Nissan Patrol, following the wheel tracks that had been left in the sand, keeping the revs of the diesel engine constant and correcting the occasional fish-tailing of the back end. After Beagle Bay, the sealed road reappeared until we came to the turn-off for Kooljaman, where we were back on a deeply rutted sand road – yellow sand this time.

Our accommodation was one of the safari tents; ours was named Nilamil, erected on a stilted wooden deck. The luxury tent had a large bedroom with two singles, a kitchen, and bathroom at the rear, at the front a wooden balustraded veranda with magnificent views overlooking the sea. We had arrived about 4.30pm on Thursday and, after unloading our cases and our shopping bags of vegetables and fruit, we headed down to the Western Beach to see the sunset. The sun goes down quickly in this part of the world, with a spectacular orange glow spreading upwards from the ocean horizon and washing into the darkening sky. A golden path of light stretched from the beach across the water, to the point where the sun was beginning to sink from our sight.

Earlier, we had rung Vincent, our Aboriginal guide, from the reception office, to ask if he would take us mud crabbing the next day.

"Yes!" he shouted, from his end of the telephone line. "Be at the turn-off for the airstrip at seven a.m. I will wait for you."

The next day was Good Friday. The sun rose just after 5.30am. Lou went for a walk along the beach while I showered and made a cup of tea.

We were only four minutes late meeting Vincent in his Suzuki Jimny. He waved hello and called out,

"Follow me."

Vincent would turn out to be a man of few words. We drove south for a few kilometres before turning left onto a narrow sand track with a roughly painted 'No Entry' symbol on a wooden post at the entrance. Vincent clambered out of his vehicle to check that our tyre pressures were sufficiently low and, after he pronounced, "Should be OK," we set off on the trail, following the Suzuki as best we could. We travelled for some time through the bush, scraping past overhanging shrubs and just succeeding in negotiating the many deep sand ruts until we stopped in front of a mangrove swamp.

Out of the Suzuki jumped two matchstick Aboriginal boys who were some of Vincent's six grandchildren. They grabbed their hooked metal rods and ran off excitedly, barefooted, into the mangrove mud, while grandfather pulled his short rubber boots on and zipped them up. Staring at our sandaled feet, he asked if we had boots.

"No," we replied, sheepishly.

"Maybe OK," he said, without conviction, and we followed him into the dark undergrowth beneath the dense mangrove canopy. "Walk on tree roots," he advised, as we sank into the mud way past our ankles.

Our flip-flop sandals disappeared from view and it took some effort to make them surface, with sucking and plopping sounds, from the mud. Eric and Josh had no such trouble, as they ran across the mud like tiny marsh sprites, followed by their grandfather at a more leisurely pace. Well behind came Lou and me struggling for balance on the wet and slippery roots, while holding on to thin mangrove tendrils that had little hope of

taking our weight in an emergency. Life was further complicated by the need to carry our hooked metal rods and, in my case, a camera too.

"One in here," shouted Eric and Josh, peering into a fallen and rotting hollow log.

We slowly got there and were instructed to poke our metal rods into the log cavities to attempt hooking the mud crab so he could be pulled out. A large pincer claw shot out of the log's entrance hole – but with no crab attached. Vincent said that the crab had thrown us one of his claws, presumably in the hope that we would settle for this prize and leave him to continue a one-armed lifestyle until he grew a replacement claw. It was 'no deal', and the crab, with its six inch wide shell, was put in the hunter's sack, together with the abandoned

claw. We caught four crabs in all but the female was released to continue her role in breeding and maintaining the mud crab population.

Finally we emerged from the stygian gloom of the undergrowth into the morning sunlight. Our clothes and faces were spattered with black mud and our legs and sandals heavily coated in a glutinous and fetid ooze. We drove to a nearby river bank, with the intention of washing off the mud. The tracks of a crocodile were seen proceeding in the direction of the river but Vincent dismissed it as a small one and led us into the water for a wash. For Lou and me it was a very rapid wash, and we quickly scrambled back up the river bank, maintaining a good look out.

"So, how big is a little crocodile?" we asked Vincent, nervously, as he later emerged from the water.

"Only four to five feet long," he replied. It was difficult to share his relaxed view of the world.

Vincent kept one crab and gave us two. We thanked them all for a great adventure and said our goodbyes.

When back at our camp, we borrowed a large saucepan from reception and Lou carried it to the shore and collected some of the crystal-clear ocean salt water. This went on the barbeque stove and she added a lime (cut into halves), fresh basil, lemon grass stalk and a red chilli pepper to make our stock. When this was boiling, the grey crabs and claws were dropped in and cooked for ten minutes, emerging with a bright red colouring.

A spinach, papaya, and macadamia nut salad dressed with olive oil and juice squeezed from a fresh orange completed our bush tucker lunch.

We dined as well as any king and his beautiful princess daughter, washing down the succulent crab meat with Redbank wheat beer from Matilda Bay.

I think one can argue that crab fully qualifies as 'fish' for a Good Friday lunch.

Canada 2009 Diary

Arrival

We were seven planes and crews gathering in Toronto for the start of a two week-flying trip around Eastern Canada. The itincrary had been planned by Canadian Clare McEwan, ably assisted by his lead pilot, Mike Brooker.

The crews were all staying at the Harbour Castle Hotel, by the side of Lake Ontario. Our check rides were completed in the local area around Toronto, and we were ready to go.

The welcome dinner was held at the prestigious Royal Canadian Military Institute, founded in 1890. The Edwardian stone building is flanked by two nineteenth century cannons, which were cast in the Woolwich Royal Arsenal in 1813 and 1815. Our table for dinner was laid in the fine library, amidst a faint aroma of antiquarian books on military matters, while the surrounding walls displayed campaign trophies including African clubs and spears amongst the more normal military regalia. Our dinner was splendid, welcome speeches given and a toast made to a safe and enjoyable flying expedition in Ontario, Quebec, and Nova Scotia.

Day One, Monday 14 September

Toronto City Airport is on an island which, whilst separated by only 400 feet of water from the mainland

at the end of Bathurst Street, requires a crossing, on the world's shortest ferry ride.

It was around eleven in the morning when the Canadian flying adventure began for 'The Intrepid British Aviators'. We had good weather, with broken clouds at 2,500 feet for our flight to Wiarton, where we waited for the low cloud base to lift at our destination, North Bay. Wiarton Airfield has named its terminal after Eileen Vollick, Canada's first lady pilot, who at the age of nineteen took off from a frozen lake in a Curtiss Jenny JN-4, fitted with skis, for her flight test, after which she was awarded Private Pilot Licence number 77.

Improving weather reports allowed the fleet to return to the air for the two hour flight across the island-spattered coastline of Georgian Bay, then over forested terrain before crossing Lake Nippissing and landing on runway 26 at North Bay.

A two hour bus ride took us to the southern shores of Lake Temagami, where we transferred onto a pontoon boat for the fifteen minute lake ride to the Ket-Chun-Eny Lodge. The log cabin-style lodge and its rustic accommodation was on island number 336 out of the some 1300 islands on the lake. Our meal that evening was an outdoor fish barbeque, a pickerel dinner with salad, whilst overlooking the lake in the evening light.

Day Two, Tuesday 15 September

The morning saw one party travelling to another island for an exploratory walk, but no bears or moose were spotted. Another group of us took a more leisurely boat ride around the islands in the southern part of this huge lake. Deryck, Robin, and Nigel elected to do some fishing from the jetty, with Deryck demonstrating his rod and line skills by landing a couple of respectable fish. Robin elected to fish in shorts, which may have frightened his fish away, and I just don't think Nigel's heart was in it at all.

After a lazy afternoon, we dressed for dinner and were ferried in the Ket-Chun-Eny pontoon water taxi to Mike and Nicole Brooker's delightful lake cottage, on island 663. Nicole, along with her charming friend Tracey from a nearby island, had prepared a sumptuous feast for us that we all enjoyed to the full.

Transport to our home island, late that evening, was a problem, as our water taxi had struck a rock during its return journey in the blackest black night, with no moonlight to guide its way. Mike and Tracey agreed to ferry us in their separate small boats using torchlight and 'back of their hand' knowledge of the lake, its

channels and rocks. I think we all found this a scary ride home and we were very pleased to get into our beds at midnight. Thank you to Captain Mike and Skipper Tracey.

Day Three, Wednesday 16 September

Our departure from North Bay was a little stressed, with the air traffic controller in the tower insisting on repeating his lengthy listing of all other aircraft on the taxiways, runway, and in the circuit to each of our seven aircraft in turn. We knew it off by heart at the end. Matters did not improve when Derek managed to direct

Paul onto the wrong taxiway, disrupting the controller's carefully laid plan of ground movements. The final straw, before the men in the white coats carried the screaming controller away, was when each of us did our power checks on the taxiway and not on the apron, breaking a rule that he said everyone knew – except, apparently, visiting pilots!

It was a relief to change to an en-route frequency as soon as we were airborne and enjoy the peace and quiet of the cockpit. We flew along the beautiful Ottawa River, which for much of its length represents the border between the Ontario and Quebec Provinces. At 3,800 feet, we were under the clouds as we flew for a landing on the westerly runway of the Ottawa Carp Airfield. We were taken by bus to the picturesque

Chateau Laurier hotel, in the city centre, alongside the Rideau Canal and across the bridge from Parliament Square.

Day Four, Thursday 17 September

Rest day in Ottawa.

A morning visit was made to the national Canadian Aviation Museum situated on the RCAF Rockcliffe Airfield. It contains a wide variety of civilian and military aircraft, representing the history of Canadian aviation from the pioneer era up to the present day. We enjoyed the collection of vintage bush planes from the 1920s through to the 1940s. We were also able to visit the separate hangar to see aircraft on which conservation and restoration work was being planned or undertaken.

Perhaps the story that grabbed our attention most was that told by Mike of the Avro Canada CF-105 Arrow, a delta-wing interceptor aircraft built in Canada, which from 1953 was designed to be one of the first supersonic planes with speeds of Mach 2 at altitudes exceeding 50,000 ft.

In 1958, and on only its third flight, the Mark I aircraft went supersonic and a top speed of Mach 1.98 was eventually reached at three-quarters throttle, using the lower-powered J75 engines. A more powerful Iroquois engine had been developed and was fitted in the Mark II aircraft, which never flew, as the development programme was cancelled in 1959 by the then Canadian Prime Minister, John Diefenbaker, for political reasons that are still debated to this day. Diefenbaker also ordered the destruction of all Arrow aircraft, engines, production tooling, and technical data. Only one nose cone and part of a wing remains, and those are in the museum. Canadian aviation does not have warm memories of John Diefenbaker.

Nearly 15,000 Avro employees were sacked and many went to the US and worked on the NASA space programme, whilst others went to Europe and became part of the BAE and Aérospatiale design teams for Concorde. What ground-breaking performance might the Mark II have achieved, one wonders.

The afternoon was spent looking around Parliament Square and exploring Ottawa, Canada's bi-lingual capital city.

Day Five, Friday 18 September

By the time we had breakfasted, travelled to the Carp Airfield, prepared our planes, and had Mike's briefing, it was almost midday before we got airborne. We flew east across the Canadian Shield, with the ski resort runs appearing as gashes in the tree-lined hills. We skirted north of the busy Montreal control zones, with the exception of Deryck and Robin, who sweet-talked the French Canadian controllers into allowing them a scenic flight over the city. After Montreal, we followed the course of the impressive Saint Lawrence River, which drains The Great Lakes into the Atlantic Ocean, and just over two hours after leaving Ottawa we were switching frequency to Quebec Tower on 118.65 for Jean Lesage International Airport. Approach procedures require flying along the south bank of the Saint Lawrence at 2000 feet, towards the two large bridges spanning the river, waiting for ATC to allow a 90 degree left turn to join downwind for runway 30.

Our hotel was another French-style chateau, this one called Frontenac, which was even bigger than the sumptuous Laurier we had just left. It is situated in the heights above the port and the Saint Lawrence River. A statue of Samuel de Champlain stood proudly on the cliff top in tribute to the founding of Quebec City by this French master mariner and explorer, who sailed from the French port of Honfleur in 1608, where a plaque commemorates his voyages to Acadia and Canada.

In the bar that evening we benefitted from Ian's encyclopaedic knowledge of Scottish malt whiskies in selecting the best available digestif, although it was noted that Simon somehow finished up with the bill for the drinks.

Day Six, Saturday 19 September

In the morning we took a bus tour of the city and the Battlefields Park, now preserved as a local amenity parkland with walking trails and outdoor concerts. Our Quebecois guide was gracious enough to attribute victory in the Battle of the Plains of Abraham to the British troops under the command of General Wolfe, who defeated the French troops and Canadian militia under the Marquis de Montcalm in 1759. It was a pivotal battle in the seven years' war over the fate of New France, influencing the later creation of Canada. Both Wolfe and Montcalm died from wounds received in the battle.

Quebec City is the capital of Quebec, Canada's largest province. The city is full of charm and style with street performers, open air cafés, good quality restaurants, shops and amazing trompe l'oeil murals on the sides of buildings.

Day Seven, Sunday 20 September

With nearly four hours flying ahead of us, we departed Quebec for Mont-Joli – curiously named, for we could see no mountain nor were we overwhelmed with the prettiness of the airfield, though it did have a coffee

machine. We ate our picnic lunch in the deserted airport terminal and read the display documenting the loss of seventeen supply vessels and five naval ships sunk by U-boats in the Saint Lawrence River during the Second World War.

Our flight to the eastern shores of Quebec took us over the coastal town of Percé, which has a long and narrow rock rising from the waters of the bay. This large dusky pink rock is topped with grass and stands isolated in the sea, joined only by a narrow natural rock path to the mainland. It has a hole at the base big enough for an elephant to pass through, should one be available, and the main rock is guarded by a sentry-like lone column of rock, the furthest from the shore.

We made our landing at the nearby airfield of Du Rocher Percé and had our photos taken for the local paper. This local airfield fleet consists of just two

homebuilts, so the arrival of our seven aircraft was big news around there.

Our hotel was comfortable, although we missed out on the legendary Canadian hospitality in the restaurant and bar. Maybe they were having a bad day, happens to all of us, or perhaps the problem was Nigel's passing resemblance to General Wolfe.

Day Eight, Monday 21 September

Our first leg took us to Prince Edward Island and Charlottetown Airfield, where we received a very warm welcome and a hot meal in the Flying Club restaurant. This served ideal food for hungry pilots: fish and chips, with thick brown gravy on the chips, and a bread roll. Who says French cuisine is not alive and well in Canada?

After refuelling, we flew over the spectacular islands of Nova Scotia, with many channels, inlets, and waterways amongst a seemingly endless carpet of evergreen and deciduous trees in the first stages of their autumn colours. Our landing was at Cape Breton Island on the gravel runway of the Crown Jewel Ranch, where we were met by a horse and cart. The cart, pulled by Sebastian, a golden draught horse from Norway, easily accommodated up to six people each trip along the woodland trail. Sebastian made an additional trip back to collect Nigel and Marie-France's luggage.

The ranch, just outside of Baddeck, is run by Nahman and Iris, both Israeli émigrés, who swapped their military careers for a tourism lifestyle, with the focus on quality accommodation and outdoor pursuits. They keep a pack of Eskimo dogs which, while they do not have the same strength as the Husky, are hardier and have superior stamina, useful for winter trekking.

Day Nine, Tuesday 22 September

Deryck, Robin, Lety, Nigel, and Marie-France chose to spend their rest day relaxing on a luxurious sailing yacht on the Bras d'Or Lake.

The Electric Spark that Jumps

The rest of the squadron took the coach trip to the historic Fortress of Louisbourg which, from 1719 until its capture in 1758, protected the fur trade and fishing businesses of New France from the British. It is now a National Historic Site. Renovation began in 1961, aided by the Canadian Government, which funded the training of local out-of-work miners to become masons and carpenters to undertake the restoration. Historians, archaeologists, engineers, and architects continue to work with the craftsmen on this site, which is inhabited by roleplaying soldiers and townsfolk in eighteen century costume. The firing of one of the cannons on the walls of the battlements was enacted in the afternoon, with a resounding "bang" and much gunpowder smoke. Roger could not fully come to terms with the equal opportunities requirements to have comely maidens (and those for whom 'comely' is now a passing memory) roleplaying some of the battle-hardened, rum-swilling French military guards. Maybe

it is not authentic, but it certainly is appealing to the discerning eye.

Baddeck is also famous for being the site of Canada's first powered flight in 1909, when the tri-wing Silver Dart, designed in part by Alexander Graham Bell (he of the invention of the telephone), lifted off from the ice on Baddeck Bay.

Day Ten, Wednesday 23 September

The weather, first thing next morning, was low cloud covering the hills, but by the time we had finished breakfast the sun was burning off the cloud and we could depart the gravel runway, one at a time, doing our power checks on the back track run. Most aircraft flew direct to Port Hawkesbury, but Robin and Lety, as well as Derek and Paul, chose to fly north to Sydney Harbour and then over the Fortress of Louisbourg before joining the others. Our refueller at Port Hawkesbury had been the Twin Otter pilot who flew into the Arctic delivering supplies supporting the attempt, in 2000, by Sir Ranulph Fiennes to walk solo to the North Pole, which failed when his sleds fell through the ice.

With a cold front advancing towards us, we elected for discretion over valour and cut out our planned scenic tour of Cape Breton Island and made direct for the Golf Resort of Fox Harb'r. We discovered that the 15-33 runway alignment was at right angles to the strong and gusting wind. Runway 33 was chosen, but it involved three aircraft making go-arounds on their first attempt before working out that the turn on finals needed to be made about half a mile early to avoid being blown way off the runway heading. Wind shear on short finals didn't help either! Probably our most 'sporty' landing of the tour, and fully tested our piloting skills.

We were accommodated in houses overlooking the golf course and our evening meal was in the luxurious clubhouse restaurant. We all had a sharp intake of breath at the three figure prices in the wine list but Kathryn, the sommelier, came up trumps selecting modestly priced yet delicious Galician white and Valpolicella Ripasso red wines to accompany our meal and settle our nerves.

Day Eleven, Thursday 24 September

Thursday was our rest day. Some of us had planned for a game of golf in the morning but the weather was foul. The rain relented after lunch and Deryck, Derek, and Ian took on the challenging course with glass-like greens and wonderful views of the sea. We had a fun round of indifferent quality golf, and for the last few holes had the dubious privilege of following a six-ball match played by a group of insurance conference delegates who had seemingly enjoyed a liquid lunch while their wives bought up nearly all of the pink outfits from the golf shop.

Robin and Paul enjoyed their own putting competition on a shiny practice green with rolling hills that could require the putt to be hit west for a hole that lay in the east.

Dinner that evening was lobster and the conversation was about our prospects for flying in the morning.

Day Twelve, Friday 24 September

We spent a classic 'waiting to fly' day reading forecast after forecast hoping for a weather window, but finally we had to stay another day. As airfield crew rooms go, the accommodation at Fox Harb'r would rate amongst some of the most pleasant.

We met and had a good chat with Ron Joyce in the bar. Born in Nova Scotia, Ron is the self-made multi-millionaire owner of this golf complex, his unashamed retirement hobby. Ron made his money when he sold the Tim Hortons chain of coffee shops to Wendy's, the US fast food chain. Ron is also a pilot and owns five aircraft, most of them being a lot larger than our fleet of single engine birds. He has also experienced the high crosswinds at his airfield when, in 2007, he survived the land short crash of his $40m Bombardier Global 5000 en route from Hamilton. Ron insists he was sitting in the back and had two professional pilots flying the monster machine. One would imagine his insurance excess has gone up a bit since that claim.

We chose to have our farewell dinner at Fox Harb'r and had tables set up in the downstairs bar and restaurant. After main course, we had our speeches thanking Clare and Mike and presenting memento gifts signed by us all. For entertainment, we chose the Monty Python song 'I'm a Lumberjack' to the words "I'm a pilot and I'm OK", with verses for each of the crews. A bold attempt was made by Derek, Robin, and Deryck to sing this in tune, with occasional success. Clare bravely endured a modified rendition of the Johnny Cash classic, 'A Boy Named Clare (Sue)'.

Day Thirteen, Saturday 25 September

At last we had perfect flying weather, with little headwind, for our five to six hour flight back to Ottawa, this time landing at the Gatineau field.

Derek Alway

We said our goodbyes to Ian, Carol, and Fiona Buchan, and also to Roger and Simon, who were taxied the five hours to Toronto so they could catch their Sunday morning flights home.

The Electric Spark that Jumps

The rest of us were staying for a third week and went to the world's largest log cabin, Chateau Montebello, with a cathedral-like central lobby and lounge with a central, many-faced stone fireplace and chimney. The chateau is an impressive spider-like structure, with five log cabin arms containing more than two hundred rustic guest rooms.

The weather forecast was most unpromising, with a belt of bad weather travelling our way from the west and looking set to keep us grounded until Wednesday at the earliest. We were looking forward so much to the float plane flying and the ride in the Lancaster Bomber – now both of these highlights were in serious doubt. We could only wait and see what the weather would bring.

Such is flying.

Derek Alway

The Lancaster Bomber

The Canadian weather had been kind to our seven light aircraft during the first week of September, whilst we flew across Ontario and Quebec, but our luck began to run thin during the second week after landing in Nova Scotia.

The Intrepid Aviators of 2009 were on a flying tour of Eastern Canada, heading north from Toronto at first then moving east until we arrived on Cape Breton Island, landing in a fierce crosswind at Fox Harbour. We had intended a two day stop but this was extended to a third day by a series of weather fronts that would have made flying dangerous for our single-engine planes. As pilot waiting rooms go, the luxurious surroundings of the Fox Harbour Country Club dulled the pain of inactivity.

The following day we were airborne again and, after arriving at Chateau Montebello, just over the Quebec border to the north of Ottawa, we were hit by a second batch of poor weather. We were told to look forward to a succession of low pressure areas, which were forecast to be with us for the first three days of our third week in Canada. Our planned visit to Rice Lake to enjoy training in 'how to fly a float plane' became a victim of the wind, rain, and miserably low cloud base. We opted to pass the time in Montreal.

Missing out on the much-anticipated opportunity to take off from and land back onto a Canadian lake was a cruel blow. Our anxieties now shifted to whether we could get back to Toronto by Wednesday evening to enjoy our planned flights in the World War II Lancaster bomber. The weather gods heard our pleas and Wednesday looked flyable, albeit with marginal conditions along the route. We returned to our planes, which were waiting for us at Ottawa Gatineau Airfield, and after reviewing aviation weather forecasts, and much discussion, the decision was made to go. We kept below 2500 feet to avoid icing conditions and either dodged the rain showers or flew right underneath, enjoying an airborne plane wash. The clouds gradually lifted as we travelled south west and we were able to include a scenic flight over Niagara Falls and get some good aerial photos.

Thursday morning was an early start to allow for rush hour traffic in the journey to Hamilton Airfield, where the Canadian Wartime Heritage Museum was located. This turned out to be a pilot's toy shop of restored and flyable historic warplanes, including the legendary four-engine Avro Lancaster bomber.

The first flight was scheduled for 10am and the briefing, for the four of us lucky enough to be on the flight, began at 9am. Ted was a retired headmaster who overflowed with pride for his pilot father, who flew DC3 Dakotas in the Burma Campaign to resupply the Allied troops fighting a bitter jungle war against the Japanese during 1944/45. Ted talked about the work of the museum in the restoration and preservation of historic aircraft. Their Lancaster, which is one of only seventeen left in the world, was built in 1945 and acquired by the museum in 1977 at a cost of C$25,000. Not a bad price for a plane that, at today's values, would have cost one and a quarter million pounds sterling to build, even if it was in a parlous state. Ten years of dedicated and skilled engineering work by volunteers were required to restore it to flying condition. This aircraft is one of only two that still flies, the other being in the UK and used for air shows and the Battle of Britain flypast over Buckingham

Palace. The Canadian Lancaster is the only one that will take members of the Museum Trust, assigned as temporary crew, for up to an hour's flight. This was a truly unique and rare opportunity.

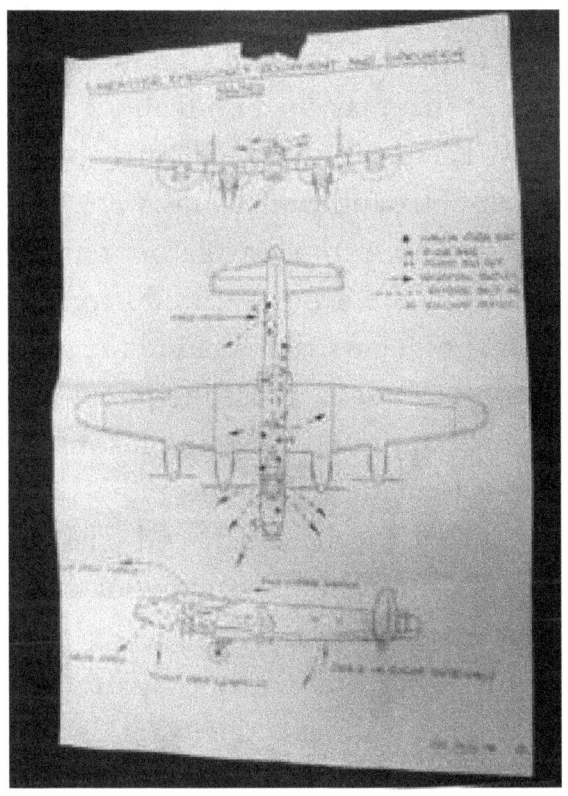

Ted made sure we understood the safety issues associated with flight in a sixty-four-year-old aircraft and asked us to sign a waiver form cancelling any future liability claim we might have against the museum. It was then time to meet the captain, co-pilot, and flight engineer and board the aircraft, with mixed emotions of excitement and nervousness.

A Lancaster bomber would have had a crew of seven during the war: the pilot in the left-hand seat on a raised platform to give maximum visibility, and to his right the flight engineer sat on a collapsible canvas seat surrounded by dials and switches monitoring the performance of the engines and aircraft systems. Below and forward of them lay the bomb aimer, face down in a transparent Perspex bubble hanging under the nose of the aircraft. His additional jobs were as a forward gunner and to assist the navigator, reporting what could be seen on the ground 20,000 feet below. The navigator sat at his chart table behind the pilot and was curtained off so as not to affect the pilot's night vision with the lights required for reading his maps. The rest of the crew was made up of the radio operator, the mid-section gunner and the 'tail-end Charlie' gunner, also in a Perspex bubble but hanging out the rear of the fuselage between the two tail fins.

For our flight we did not anticipate the need for three anti-aircraft gunners. Our captain for the day was Andy Dobson, the right-hand seat occupied by Leon Evans, acting as co-pilot, and Craig Brookhouse was the flight engineer, in his position behind the captain's seat. All radio communications were handled by the captain. We, the temporary bomber crew members, had four seats, one behind the other along the port side of the fuselage, each with a small rectangular observation window at eye-line height.

The interior of the aircraft can fairly be described as spartan at best, with raw metal girders exposed, uniform olive drab paintwork and various metallic obstacles across the width of the fuselage. It was a functional aircraft designed by Roy Chadwick of AV Roe, the British aircraft manufacturer later absorbed into Hawker Siddeley Aviation. This plane was built for the serious, specialist, and highly risky job of night bombing runs over the then-enemy skies of Germany, Poland, and Romania.

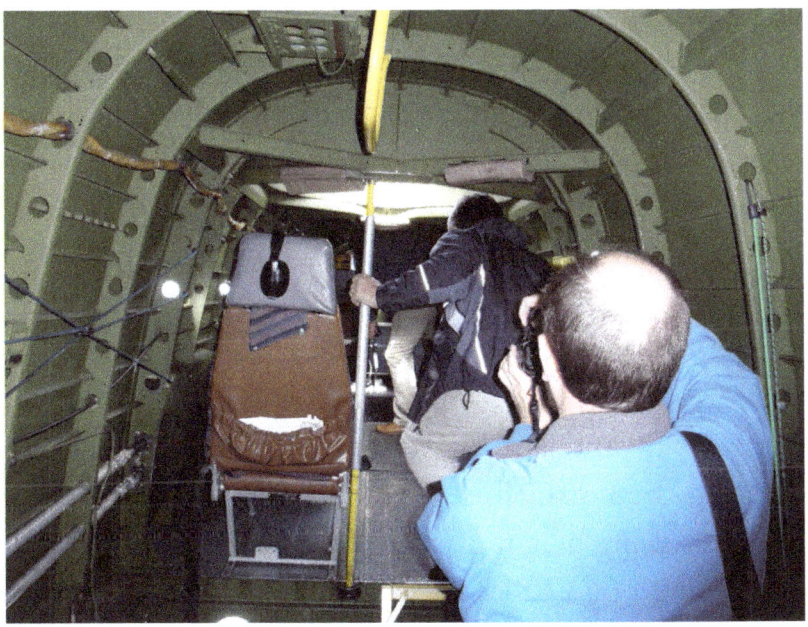

Already more than a little excited, we strapped ourselves in and listened to the outer starboard engine start up. The Merlin engine used in the Lancaster is the same as that fitted in the single-engine Spitfire fighter and has a most characteristic sound destined to quicken one's pulse. We had four Merlin engines! The second engine to fire up was the inboard starboard and, slowly, all four engines leapt into life, in sequence, each emitting an initial cloud of grey, oily smoke. We had ear protectors to wear but initially listened as the engines started up and purred in unison while the pre-flight checks were being completed. At last we began our taxi and the captain turned the aircraft into wind for the power checks. No more delays, it was time to put the ear defenders on our heads.

Films of World War II show the Lancaster as a huge aircraft, with its 102 feet wingspan dwarfing the 37 feet wingspan of the Spitfire fighter. And indeed, it was large for its day, but its fuselage is barely tall enough for a standing man and you can just about touch the sides with your outstretched arms. In turn, today's jumbo jets make this piston-engine legend look very small.

We took off at 10:21am to the north west, from runway 30, and headed towards Toronto city centre, tracking the north shore of Lake Ontario. We climbed to our cruising height of only 900 feet, flying at a gentle cruise speed of 170 knots, well short of the Lancaster's maximum speed of 240 knots in level flight. It was time for the first two of the guest crew, Deryck and Robin, to be invited up to the cockpit. Peter and I enjoyed the ride, watching the passing landscape and lake views from our observation windows and taking turns to stand

and look out of the mid-turret Perspex dome, still sporting the twin barrels of its Browning machine guns, no longer required to fight off enemy aircraft. Our cameras and heartbeats worked overtime.

It was not difficult to imagine a wartime crew of twenty-something or even teenage airmen trained and setting off for a bombing raid over the Ruhr Valley. This cigar tube was so noisy that conversation would not have been possible without an intercom. These men would climb as high as possible, 20,000 to 23,000 feet, avoiding collision with other bombers in the wave, vigilant against attacks from German fighters, flying through the flak of anti-aircraft batteries and hoping not to be illuminated by enemy searchlights. Thirty sorties made up a tour of duty, and only one in six airmen was expected to survive their first tour. These were not great odds for these courageous young men, and the odds worsened to one in forty for surviving two tours.

It is cold at 20,000 feet, especially with temperamental heating in the aircraft. The boys wrapped up in sheepskin jackets and gloves but the mid-upper and tail gunners had no aircraft heating and wore electrically-heated flying suits. Any failure in the electrical supply meant frostbite at best and a frozen demise at worst.

We have to hold these young men's bravery in the highest regard.

Robin and Deryck relinquished their places and Peter and I were able to go to the cockpit. This was easier said than done. Whilst one could step over the mid-section spar, climbing over the main spar, which held the wings onto the aircraft, was a totally different challenge, especially when you are no longer nineteen years old or supple. The technique involved lifting one's bum high to sit on the top of the spar then lifting each leg over one at a time, with much help from one's arms, whilst having your head bent forward between the knees. And we weren't wearing bulky flying suits and parachutes!

We got to stand right behind the pilots, with the flight engineer kindly giving up his place for us. The pilot's control yoke resembled the steering wheel of a car with the top half cut away. The instrument dials were very familiar from the cockpits of our single-engine planes, which are also based on designs from the 1940s. The one anachronistic addition was the Garmin 296 satellite navigation unit – a sensible addition and again familiar from our single-engine Cherokee and Cessna cockpits. In this cockpit, what was truly different were the three panels of engine management dials and switches on the starboard side behind the co-pilot's seat, which were providing a real-time health check on the aircraft engines and systems. Looking sideways out of the cockpit window, the four Merlin engines looked surprisingly close, but permitted easy visual confirmation of their smooth running.

The Electric Spark that Jumps

We had turned south from below the level of the Toronto skyscrapers, within what seemed like touching distance from the CN Tower, and climbed to 2500 feet as we made the 35 mile crossing of Lake Ontario. Approaching the southern shore, we smoothly gained additional altitude to the 3500 feet minimum level for fixed wing planes orbiting over Niagara Falls. Fluffy white clouds required a further climb to 4500 feet, which gave us tantalising glimpses of the Horseshoe Falls between the cloud gaps.

Returning to Hamilton, we made a low pass over the airfield in front of the observation platform, followed by a climbing turn with a steep angle of bank close to 60 degrees. Heart-racing exhilaration for us four pilots.

The Lancaster landed back on runway 24, as the wind had moved around and these tail draggers do not enjoy crosswind landings. We touched down at 11:07 with an airborne time of forty-six minutes, giving us close to the hour for chocks to chocks.

The Lancaster may have landed but our minds were still in the air. Our exhilarated bodies disembarked and we walked round the aircraft before shaking hands with the captain and his crew. It was time to line up alongside Kilo Bravo 726, our Lancaster Bomber, for the photo session with the crew. Was it expensive? Absolutely, but a better way for a pilot to spend C$2,000 is very hard to imagine. Truly, it was a ride of a lifetime.

The Electric Spark that Jumps

Of the 7,377 Lancaster Bombers built and flown on 156,000 sorties from 1942 to 1945, almost half were destroyed and, painfully, more than 22,000 men's lives were sacrificed. It is exhilarating to fly in this iconic bomber, whilst at the same time humbling to remember the thousands of young men whose lives were prematurely extinguished serving their country in such aircraft, helping to preserve the freedom that I can enjoy today. Gentlemen, I salute your bravery and sacrifice. You may never have heard our thanks yet you remain, always, in our grateful memories.

An Angel Watches Over Me

Our family holiday in North Devon was nearing its end. Lou and Paul had said their goodbyes on the Thursday afternoon so that they could catch their Friday flight back to Australia. Oskar needed to get back to school and Scarlet required a full month to prepare for her sixth birthday. All the grandchildren had played so beautifully together. Zach and Scarlet had bonded and even slept in the same bed, on occasions, like an old married couple. Oskar and Libs became firm friends, while Jess, in transition from childhood to young teenage beauty,

provided the elder sister role. Baby Alanis happily enjoyed extra cuddles from Auntie Lou, Libs, and Jess, but on her occasional visits to Grandad she never let her mummy get out of her sight for a moment.

It was touching to see the grandchildren hug goodbye to each other, listen to Zach's farewell speech and watch Jess give Oskar an affectionate kiss on his cheek, which he enjoyed with a faint blush.

Simon, Tracey, and family plus Grandad still had another full day at Thornwidger Barn before departing on Saturday morning. We decided to visit Clovelly, the quaint Cornish village with steep pebble-cobbled hill down to the small protected harbour.

Having been before, some years earlier, I should not have been surprised that there is now an entrance fee to visit the village. A large visitor centre has been erected at the top of the hill, where your entrance fee is paid. Children are given a fun puzzle and a pencil to play 'I Spy' as they walk through the village. The way into the village is through a vast shop selling books, photos, a myriad of tourist paraphernalia and the flimflammery that appeals to young children plus, of course, sweets, more sweets, and take-away food.

The Electric Spark that Jumps

I had not realised, or remembered, that Clovelly is owned by one family, the Hamlyns, who bought the estate in 1738. No doubt it is held in trust these days else it would, by now, be owned by the government and run by civil servants on highly inflated salaries, with the skills to turn a profitable business into an additional black hole of debt. After indignant articles in the press, this problem would, no doubt, be solved by turning the village into homes for asylum seekers or additional space for our overcrowded prisons.

All the quaint fishermen's cottages are now rented. The donkey stables are at the top of the hill, reminding us of the history of using donkeys to carry supplies on their backs, up and down the hill, until the 1990s. Nowadays deliveries are made on wooden sledges.

One third of the way down the hill we found a lady, sitting on her porch, with an eleven-week-old owl sitting on her gloved hand. She was happy for Zach to join her on the porch for a closer look. Both the owl and Zach were very wary of each other! The owl was called Pippin. Being a big fan of Tolkien, the lady has named all of her owls after characters from The Lord of the Rings, so already has a Bilbo Baggins and a Frodo in her aviary.

As we found ourselves right outside the bar of The New Inn, it would have been impolite not to sample some of the local ales in preparation for the further descent. And the plan worked, as it kept us going until two thirds of the way down, where we stopped for Devon cream teas in the cafe. Planning is so important.

The Electric Spark that Jumps

The tide was out so the curved arm of the harbour wall looked way too tall above the muddy sea bed, with the boats stranded like beached whales. Libs and I decided to walk on the pebble beach to the water's edge, for a game of throwing stones into the sea. Tracey and Simon, with Alanis strapped to his chest in her front-facing sling, led Jess and Zach to the end of the harbour wall, from where they could wave, from on high, to the pebble-throwing competitors.

Simon and Libs declined the ride back, up a side street in the Land Rover, as they were in training for the three thousand feet climb of the Lake District's Helvellyn Mountain on Sunday. Grandad bravely agreed to keep them company, but at a more measured pace. He had no plans to join the ascent on Helvellyn.

At the top of the hill we found two donkeys waiting for visitors to pat them and take photos. Toby, now blind, was content for Libs, with her featherweight frame, to sit on him and be photographed. Enquiring of the lady handler the name of the other donkey, she replied with a smile that he was called 'Donk'. Clearly a name that did what it said on the tin! Jana, the handler, was a Canadian from the north west territories, and our conversation veered towards flying.

Her dad, fabulously named 'Texas', had just had to relinquish his pilot's licence at the age of 84 and was not at all happy about that. He sounded an interesting pioneer of a man, who had flown all his life around the Yukon and northern Canada. I promised to send him my account of our flying trip around eastern Canada, although this might be tame reading for such a daring man.

Having flown over the ruins of Tintagel Castle on our way back from the Scilly Isles a year or two ago, I was keen to see it from the ground. It was only thirty miles away, although the narrow lanes of Devon and Cornwall do tend to slow down one's traveling speed. I arrived in Tintagel to find that access to the castle ruins was a half mile walk downhill, along a dirt track, to the coast. Not surprisingly, this legendary birthplace of King Arthur was a popular tourist location and had its own visitor centre and entrance ticket booth. The ruins are built on rocky cliffs that are now almost an island, linked only tenuously to the mainland, so wooden flights of steps had been constructed for the steep climb to the castle.

I was, regrettably, running short on time, since we had a table booked for six o'clock that evening, and so I reluctantly decided against a further hill climb of half an hour or more. I convinced myself that it would save time if I opted for a ride up the hill in the coastguard's Land Rover. It had nothing to do with wishing to avoid another mountain training exercise – of course! I apologised for having only a £20 note for the £1.50 fare but the cheerful driver was happy to oblige with the change. Tucking the wallet back into my side pocket, I hauled my tired legs up and onto the back seat for the bumpy four-wheel climb to the car park at the top.

I arrived back at Thornwidger Barn with only moments to spare. It was while I was changing my trousers and shirt that I realised I could not find my wallet. As happens, I searched every likely place not once but three or four times, with the same empty result. Ah well, worse things happen at sea. All that was required was to cancel the credit cards and, with some inconvenience, it would all be sorted. I was, however, sad to lose my ostrich skin wallet, which was a treasured possession, bought in Swakopmund on safari in Namibia.

Our meal, at The Cranford Arms, was excellent, and the children were very well-behaved. At the back of my mind, the lost wallet rankled. I remembered last using it to pay the coastguard for his lift, so either it must have fallen out of my pocket in his Land Rover or dropped to the floor when I descended from my seat. Alternatively, maybe it fell out in the car park as I got into 'The Silver Hornet'. I left a voicemail message with the closed police station at Bude, which would not reopen until Monday, after the weekend.

As I was getting ready for bed I became anxious that, if the wallet had been stolen, I might find myself responsible for the cost of some petty criminal's new HD television and other ill-gotten purchases. I got dressed again and drove to the top of the hill, where an Orange signal was available for my mobile phone. I got through immediately to Allied Irish Bank, who efficiently cancelled and reordered my credit and debit cards. Same story with American Express, but not so with Barclaycard. They took twelve minutes to answer my emergency call then were unable to find any record of me on the computer files. Mr. Inder Gill, from the Mumbai Call Centre, suggested I go into a branch of Barclays Bank tomorrow, Saturday, and report the loss!

I arose early the next morning and packed and loaded my car for the journey home. I intended first to drive back to Cornwall and visit Tintagel, in the faint hope that the same coastguards or the car park attendant may be there and have some news. No matter this journey would take me thirty-five miles further away from home. Tracey kindly cooked me breakfast and readily agreed to tidy up the barn and hand over the keys to Joanna, the owner who lived next door.

As I drove into the centre of Tintagel, out of the corner of my eye I spotted two coastguard Land Rovers parked in a side road. I left my car nearby but, although the driver's windows were wound down, there was no sign of anyone. I decided to ask in the nearby shop just as a man emerged from the doorway and proceeded to walk away from me, into the town.

"Excuse me," I called after him, "would you know where the coastguard drivers would be?" The man turned around; he looked familiar.

"Yes," he said, "it's me, and you have lost a wallet."

My heart rate quickened considerably as I waited for what he had to say next. He apologised for looking in (what I was hoping was) my wallet for identification.

"That's fine," I gulped, as he said,

"You are a pilot."

Then I knew, for sure, it was my wallet, as it contained my Flight Crew identity card. I am not sure how many times I said "thank you," but I do remember shaking his hand at least three separate times, very warmly. He walked with me to his Land Rover, leant inside and retrieved my ostrich skin wallet from his glove box and handed it to me. I felt totally overwhelmed and my vision was becoming blurred from the tears welling up in my eyes. I managed to remember my manners and gave him a £20 note for the coastguard's charity box. What an amazing piece of serendipitous luck that the very first person in Tintagel I should speak to was the man who found, and saved, my wallet.

Although my grandfather, a cabinet maker by trade, moved to Dorset, he never lost his Devon accent and was nicknamed by his work mates as 'Devon'. Some part of me must be Devonian, and it was a good feeling to be amongst those West Country men, who radiate friendliness, honesty, and integrity.

As I drove away, I could not resist emitting a loud, wild yelp of relief and delight that left a puzzled look on the faces of passers-by. Silently, and with moist eyes, I also gave grateful thanks to my guardian angel, who continues to take care of me, although she has been out of our reach for more than twenty years now. We all need someone to watch over us and I am a lucky man to have mine.

Strangely, it turned out to be another stroke of luck, or good celestial management, that Barclaycard had no record of me, since my Visa card still worked in the cash machine. Perhaps with a touch more luck, the billing department will lose my records too.

Libs and Simon climbed Helvellyn on Sunday. It took them five and a half hours, up and down, in varying inclement weather conditions. What a tough challenge for an eight-year-old girl to conquer. Well done, Libs, we are all so proud of you. Perhaps one day, I will have a mountaineer for a grandchild. My guardian angel will be getting even less of an opportunity for a sit down with a cup of tea if that is the case.

Closing the Loop

MARCH 19 TO APRIL 6 2012

Derek Alway

Closing the Loop

What Loop is That?

It was unfinished business really, so when the opportunity arose we booked our place at once.

It was in 2005 that Paul Edwards and I joined a group of five light aircraft, all Cessna 172s, from Goana Air Safaris, led by the capable and entertaining Captain Keith Fearnside. We flew around the top half of Australia. We started in Perth and followed the coastline of Western Australia northwards, visiting Cervantes with its famous Pinnacle Desert, Coral Bay and Port Hedland to see the large ocean tankers load up with iron ore and where all the buildings in the town are covered in red ferric dust. We savoured Broome, the pearling capital of the world with the art deco open-air cinema, then on to Derby, famous for the Prison Tree, a hollow boab with a steel grille used as a lock up and less famous for the messy and destructive flocks of fruit bats.

Following the coastline as it curved to the north east, we rested at the diamond mining area of Kununurra before a two day stop-over in the Kakadu National Park, just south east of Darwin. From there we continued, gradually steering south easterly across the top of Northern Territory, just below the Gulf of Carpenteria into Queensland, to the gold rush town of Charters Towers, now a spectre of itself in its glory days, before meeting the Pacific coast south of Cairns, from where we flew to a fun landing, the runway along the water's edge on Brampton Island in the Whitsundays. Miss that runway and one had to fly around the close-by Cockermouth Island to get back on finals for Brampton.

Our trip concluded sixteen days after we set off from Perth, at Redcliffe Airfield, our destination just north of Brisbane.

Getting Ready

Now it was 2012 and we were to finish the circumnavigation, restarting at Brisbane to continue our clockwise coastline route to Jandakot Airport, just to the south of Perth, from where we last took off on the 24th September 2005. Goana was no longer in business, having been overwhelmed by the drop in business after the 9/11 atrocities in New York, but also by the bureaucratic over-reaction in Australia, with ensuing paperwork and regulatory overkill, much of it designed by people who seemed to have little or no knowledge of aviation.

I had been in Australia for three weeks, spending precious family time with my daughter Louise, her husband Paul, and my two Australian grandchildren, Oskar, who is eleven, and Scarlet, who is seven. Now, Monday 19th March, it was time to fly to Brisbane with Queensland and Northern Territory Aerial Services or, as they are better known, Qantas. The weather was hot and humid in Brisbane and thunderstorms had been around all week. I checked into the Regis Park Hotel on the North Quay banks of the Brisbane River, overlooking the Victoria Bridge. My co-pilot on our adventure, Paul Edwards, had arrived earlier that morning from London and crashed out in his room. I explored the city on my own, with the main objective of finding a good restaurant for our evening meal. Paul finally awoke at 4.30 in the afternoon, looking like a sleep-deprived zombie. 'Have I chosen well in my co-pilot?' I wondered, as there seemed to be room for a marked improvement.

Dinner was at an excellent steak restaurant, the Moo Moo Grill, at the corner of Edward and Margaret Streets. It has the strap line of 'Moo Moo is a rare steak restaurant, well done'. And it was.

The next day we were met by the Canadian owner of Air Safaris International, Clare McEwan, who had planned and organised the circumnavigation flight around Australia, of which we were doing the southern half. Paul and I already knew Clare from the memorable Canadian flying safari that he organized for us in 2009. Clare had, a few years back, decided on a mid-life career change from working in the aluminium industry to planning and running flying safaris, starting in Australia where the weather is generally more predictable than in Canada. It was a courageous decision, but he is his own boss, the founder, CEO, president, CFO, supremo, general factotum, lord high executioner, tea boy, and odd-job man, as befits a small start-up business. His business grows steadily, helped now by his wife Helen, as he adds further routes in Canada and France, whilst researching others. He has that Canadian good humour, tolerance, and patience that is required of a tour director, sitting on top of a foundation of determination and creativity required to solve the many unexpected problems that can and do occur.

As we entered the minibus, we were introduced to one of the other pilots, Doug Mitten, also Canadian, who astounded us by revealing he was eighty-three years old and still flying his float plane back home in Ontario.

We set off for the two hour journey to Toowoomba, which would gradually take us on the climb up to the Darling Downs on the western slopes of the Great Dividing Range, which, despite its name, was only 2,300 feet above sea level at this point. We stopped on the way to collect the 'Swiss Family Wiedmann', Martin and Barbara and their three-year-old son, Willy. The Wiedmanns had slightly more luggage than one would find in an average house move, but did explain that this was because they were away from home for three months.

So with an age range in our group from three to eighty-three I was feeling rejuvenated and barely middle-aged.

On arrival in Toowoomba, scene of horrific flash flooding in 2011, when cars were swept away and eight people sadly lost their lives, we checked into the Burke & Wills Hotel. The afternoon and the next day were spent at the Darling Downs Aero Club for a briefing by lead pilot, Graham King, and flying check rides. Graham learnt to fly in 1961, being sixteen at that time, and had been the President of Darling Downs Aero Club for many years, as well as a flying instructor. He is retired from his profession as a lawyer, having become frustrated with the increasingly aggressive, confrontational style of legal work these days. His role as the flight director was to keep us safe and alive and ensure that we flew in accordance with the rules and laws of Australian aviation. To this end, Graham worked diligently in preparation of flight documentation and gave us clear and detailed briefings. A demanding job that was delivered with the right result – we all made it and enjoyed the journey along the way.

We were introduced to Dick Kleeman, a retired commercial pilot who would be flying with Martin Wiedmann as a safety pilot. Martin is an experienced pilot but because of the differences in the aircraft he was flying, together with responsibility for his family, he wisely sought the help of a local pilot while flying over this different terrain.

Graham's briefing introduced us to the mysteries of Australian aviation charts, of which there are many. The 1 to 1 million scale WAC charts gave good geographical information but sadly did not contain any aviation data other than the location of aerodromes – which, it is true, is good information to have when you are flying! So to address this famine of aviation information it was also important to have the Visual Navigation Charts (VNC), at 1 to 1/2 million scale, which gave airspace data and navigation aids but, strangely, still no airfield approach information or radio frequencies for communication. For that, one needed the Visual Terminal Charts (VTC) at 1 to 1/4 million scale, but these must be used in conjunction with the ERSA (En Route Supplement Australia) which was a 976 page book full of important information. Confused?? We were, and you will be too, as we also had the En Route Low Airways charts, the General Flying Guides for the major city airports and the weather area maps. What could be simpler other than, of course, having one chart and one book, such as those we use to fly around Europe? Dick drily noted that we probably had more charts in each aircraft than Captain Cook had aboard the Endeavour on his journey from Whitby, arriving at Botany Bay in 1770.

We were more than ready for our evening meal, which was kindly provided by Les and Jenny Louis, who were friends of Graham and Noni King. Jenny and Noni produced an outstanding meal, complemented with fine Australian wines selected by Les, who clearly has an alternative career awaiting him as a sommelier.

The following day we learned about the many things that could kill us in Australia and how to survive a forced landing in the wilds of the country, each armed with only a machete, water transpiration kit for obtaining water from a bush, our fishing line and hooks, plus signalling mirrors to summon help. We were also warned to check outside toilets before sitting on them, else one might have a cold and clammy surprise in the nether regions from a green frog leaping out of its home under the rim of the bowl.

Our aircraft were allocated and Paul and I had Cessna 172S Victor Hotel – Charlie Echo Victor which turned out to be a lovely plane. Graham took each of us out for a check flight in VH-CEV and asked us to do various tight turns, stalls and landings, and go-arounds. The aircraft and examiner survived the experience so Paul and I were given the aircraft keys. Doug was checked on Cessna 182 VH-MST, which he would be flying with Graham in the front seat and Clare as the rear seat passenger. Martin would fly the Cessna 205 VH-RYB, which would have Dick up front and Barbara and Willy in the rear seats.

Thursday 22 March was supposed to be our departure day, but the sky closed in with thick low clouds and threatened thunder on our journey. So we got to know our travelling companions better.

Doug had recently completed the sale of his plastics business. He started it and grew it into a successful international business, providing vinyl side panels for the cladding of houses. He didn't really want to sell or leave the business, even though at eighty-three it was a far cry from early retirement. He loved his business, he loved the people he worked with, but he could not find a successor and reluctantly agreed to sell to a larger company. We had a number of conversations discussing whether he made the right decision. One good outcome is Doug's eleven grandchildren and five great grandchildren have more financial security now than most Canadian youngsters.

Martin has German nationality, lives in Switzerland and is a recently retired foreign exchange banker. His wife, Barbara, is Swiss, with both Italian and German flavouring and, like Martin and many Swiss, seems to switch languages with effortless fluency. Am I jealous? You bet I am!! Barbara is also a retired Swiss banker and both of them are enjoying their good fortune and the purchasing power of the Swiss Franc against just about every other currency in the world right now. Both are good company, generous, and devoted parents of young Willy, who has yet to add a third language to his German and Italian. Willy was a bright boy, creative in his play, whiling away the many long journey hours with his iPad or sleeping. Of course, he was only three, so occasional frustration was vented with tears, but these times were few and, after all, something a three-year-old is licensed to do.

Dick is a walking example of the good-natured, adaptive, and cheerful Aussie. His relaxed and jovial exterior masked an aviator of many years' experience, whose observations were pertinent and to whom it was well worth listening when he was proffering his knowledgeable advice. Dick flew the DC9 for Australian Airlines which, after a turbulent industrial relations dispute, became consumed by Qantas in 1996. This politically charged demise of Australian Airlines in favour of Qantas still left an unhealed wound in Dick's pride.

With plenty of time on our hands we made our way through the seemingly endless rain to visit the small but interesting Zuccoli Aircraft Collection of War Birds.

Back at the Burke & Wills Hotel I was fascinated to see posters for Brophy's Famous Boxing Tent. The last time I saw a boxing tent was in the 1950's at Poole Fair, which pitched up each year on the site between the railway station and the stadium, home to the Poole

Pirates speedway team. Brophy's was the last surviving travelling boxing show, which pitched up in towns across Australia, providing opportunity to the local brawlers (and young bucks out to impress their Sheilas) to display their pugilistic skills against the professional boxers from the show. Challengers could earn $30 for every minute of the fight if they won.

"If they draw, they get nothing," owner Fred Brophy said, and, "if they lose, they get the experience."

My plan was to be Paul's manager and enter him in the heavyweight category. We could have been $300 up on the deal but were thwarted when the weather improved and we had to leave town before savouring victory.

As you will have guessed from my money-making idea with the boxing tent, Paul is a tall and powerfully-built man. Add to that his Yorkshire grit (a polite term for not knowing when to back off) and you'll be forming a mental picture of the man. Paul is legendary for taking up flying to save money!! Before that time, he built and tuned Porsche engines then raced the cars with great success, for himself and his well-stocked trophy cabinet, leaving little to console his opponents. He has developed his flying skills with the same attention to detail that was required as a racing driver and, to add jam on the bread, he understands engines, filling a gaping hole in my knowledge set. A good man to fly with but you can never get behind him in the queue to buy a round of drinks!!

On our way

At last, on Friday 23 March, we set off, a day behind schedule, in glorious sunshine. We left Darling Downs with Paul in the P1 seat and myself responsible for radio calls, navigation, and librarianship duties of the myriad charts. It was good to be flying at last, particularly as we reached the coast at Porpoise Point, turning south to fly at one thousand feet along the aptly named Gold Coast, admiring the endless yellow sand beaches fringing the blue, blue waters of the Coral Sea, all bathed in sunshine.

Almost two hours of flying and it was time to stop for a picnic lunch. Our airfield at Evans Head was a tarmac strip and a deserted hut, but Paul's landing

was observed by an appreciative audience of wallabies lining the grass verges alongside the runway.

The afternoon flight to Port Macquarie was with me at the controls and Paul assuming the navigation and radio roles. In fairness, it was not an overly demanding job as there was no-one to talk to on the radio and navigation consisted of making sure the blue bit remained on the port side of the aircraft. The sun shone all day. We had forgotten about the cold and the rain in Toowoomba and were starting to complain about how hot it was here! Not easy to keep pilots happy, especially the Whinging Pom variety.

We settled into our hotel at Port Macquarie overlooking the Hastings River, enjoying the view amongst the endless chattering of the rainbow lorikeets settling down in the tress for the evening. Along the river came the unusual sight of a group of twenty or more youngsters lying belly down on their surfboards, kicking their legs in the air as they practised paddling the boards using only their arms. This is an essential skill required when making one's way out to sea with your surfboard, through the incoming breaking waves.

Sydney Harbour

It was Saturday and we had a big day ahead of us, with the chance to fly around Sydney Harbour. We had an early breakfast followed by a long briefing in the empty bar of the hotel. Unusually for Australia, where you can be out of radio range and far away from civilisation for much of the time, this day we were in the busy area of Sydney, with many control zones to transit and radio frequency changes with associated broadcast messages, on top of which Graham required us to report at designated locations with details of where we were, the time of arrival, altitude, and estimate for the next reporting point.

Our first control zone was Williamstown military, identified as 'Willy' with true Aussie preference for the diminutive form of a word. We obtained clearance to fly coastline at five hundred feet above the sea, with the requirement to report at 'Nobbies' – Nobby's Head. We flew past Newcastle and south towards the Central Coast, where my daughter, Lou, and family live. I was in the navigator seat, busily switching charts, changing radio frequencies, obtaining clearances, and reporting our position. Paul was flying the aircraft. I identified beaches as we went by – The Entrance and Tuggerah Lake, near to Wyong (where Lou works for Mars Foods), Terrigal Beach, then Avoca Beach, which is the next one to Copacabana Beach (which Lou's house overlooks). I sent a text to Lou from the plane and told her that we would orbit their house.

Paul completed an orbit over the area where I believed they were, but it was difficult to see them on their deck because of the covering trees. I got a text saying they had a good view of us and Scarlet wanted to know if we could drop sweets from the plane!

Back on mission, we continued to Sydney, flying along the Victor One Coastal Route southbound at five hundred feet. To avoid aerial collisions, northbound traffic on the route flies at one thousand feet. I now requested to fly the Harbour Scenic One visual route and received clearance at one thousand five hundred feet. We were instructed to fly the route from Long Reef direct to the Harbour Bridge. We could make two left-hand orbits remaining east of the bridge, north of the Opera House, and west of Garden Island Naval Base, and we did just that. It was very exciting and hard to imagine being allowed to do the same thing over Tower Bridge and Saint Paul's Cathedral in London. My

camera was as busy as was possible whilst doing everything else, and Paul was fully occupied flying the plane, but we were exhilarated.

Our exit was to return to the coast, north over Manly Beach, before descending to five hundred feet back at Long Reef, making a 180 degree turn to continue south on Victor One, past Bondi Beach and Botany Bay, onto our first landing of the day after an adrenaline-fuelled morning.

Wollongong is home to the Historic Aircraft Restoration Society, where we planned a peek into their hangars. As we ate our picnic lunch, we were delighted to see that the iconic DC3 Dakota, of Berlin Airlift fame, was being taxied out of the hangars along with the STOL (short take-off and landing) Canadian de Havilland Caribou aircraft used for tactical military transport in the sixties and seventies, seeing service during the Vietnam War.

As if that wasn't good enough, then appeared the Super Constellation, with its classic triple tail fins, and known affectionately as 'Connie'. Howard Hughes ordered Constellation aircraft for TWA and inaugurated the transatlantic passenger route in 1946, competing with the PanAm Clipper service using the slower and unpressurised Sikorsky flying boats. Soon, Connies and Super Connies were flying the long haul routes around the world until its four eighteen cylinder radial propeller engines were rendered obsolete by the introduction of the jet engine in the fifties. The three aircraft were on their way to an air show and, in turn, they backtracked runway 16 and took off while we stood, watched, and photographed these beautiful planes. Not a sight one gets many opportunities to see.

The second flight of the day, with myself in the driving seat, was to the capital city of Canberra. Australians, being unable to resolve the argument between Sydney and Melbourne for capital city status, opted for the small town between the two, not on the coast but in the mountains of the Great Dividing Range, hence unifying opinion by making everyone equally unhappy with the choice. Shame they didn't move a bit more west, then they could have had Wagga Wagga, which would be much more fun for a capital city name and would have placed their capital on the delightful-sounding Murrumbidgee river.

For the hour and a half flight inland we needed to climb to six thousand feet to get over the mountains and reduce the turbulence. Poor Barbara was suffering with an unusual bout of air sickness that day so did not enjoy her scenic flight. Now home to the nation's parliament and politicians, all wisely spending their electorates' money, the town is known to Australians as 'Bullshit City'. It certainly does not lack for expensive restaurants funded by expense accounts, but we chose to eat at the hotel's Italian restaurant, enjoying a meal cooked by South East Asian chefs and served by Chinese and Rumanian waitresses. It somehow lacked the authentic 'Trattoria Italiana' experience, but... what an amazing day we had had.

Australian Capital Territory

Opinions vary on whether Canberra is an interesting place for tourists. We only had a morning in Canberra as we were keen to recoup our lost day in Toowoomba and get back on schedule. We decided to visit the Canberra War Memorial and museum, which turned out to be an excellent decision. The war memorial is on a hill at the end of a long avenue of eucalyptus trees. The avenue is coloured earth red and has white stone-bordered memorial gardens for the Australian servicemen who lost their lives fighting for their country. At the far end of this long avenue is Parliament House, affording the politicians a direct view of the memorial and acting as a constant reminder of the tragic consequences of their decisions, which one hopes will prick their consciences and help focus their minds on the loss and pain of warfare.

The museum had excellent displays and dioramas of the involvement of Australian troops in the First World War, with its ill-fated Gallipoli campaign, the Second World War, Korea, and Vietnam, amongst other conflict zones. It was sobering to see the desperate life of the trenches in France between 1914 to 1918. The topographical model of the Turkish mountains showing the Gallipoli landings defies

belief that men were asked to scale these steep cliffs and mountains with the well-prepared Turkish army sitting on the high ridges and raining down their deadly fire.

We were, not surprisingly, drawn to the aviation section of the museum, which contained aircraft from both world wars and a captured Japanese miniature submarine that was one of three to enter Sydney Harbour. The displayed Lancaster bomber, 'G' for George, was crewed by Australians and took part in many bombing raids over Germany. There was a nine minute film of wartime footage of a 500 bomber raid over Berlin, in which 50 aircraft and their crews were lost. It was a scary and sobering glimpse into the terrifying experiences that bomber crews were subjected to night after night. Brave, brave young men.

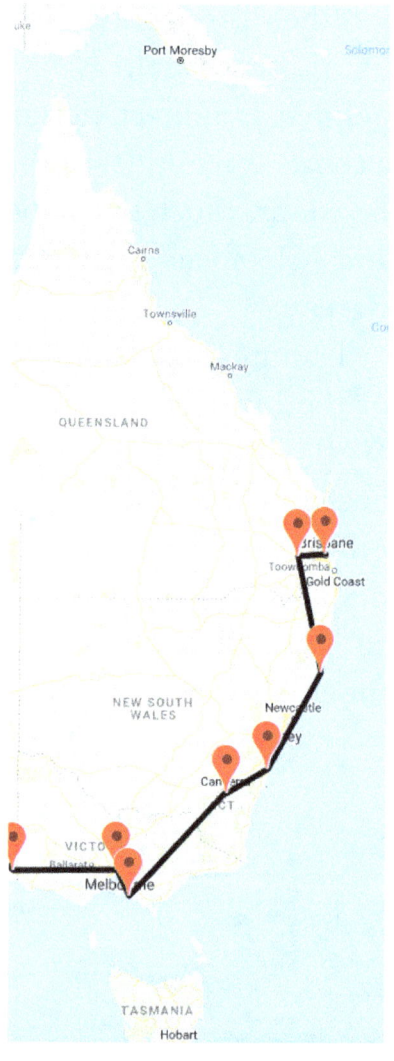

New Zealander Peter Jackson, who is famous for The Lord of the Rings, had created a film re-enacting a First World War aerial battle in the skies over France. Jackson rebuilt many aircraft, both German and Allied, of that time, using original plans, and these were used to film a dogfight between Australian and German squadrons. It was brilliantly done. It was also a reminder of the fate of an airman when the plane was shot down. As the top brass of the day denied these young men any parachutes, to discourage cowardice of jumping out of a serviceable aircraft, their dreadful decision was to burn to death in their plane as they plunged earthwards or jump out of the cockpit to their death.

Martin and Barbara decided that Willy would prefer to let off steam running around one of the parks in Canberra, which proved a good decision. They were amused by signs in the park warning Australians to beware as 'Europeans Wasps in Area'. Australians had better take care when visiting Europe, as we have lots and lots more European wasps over there!

After returning to the airfield, we embarked on the three-hour flight to Phillip Island. So it was that we left ACT, re-entered New South Wales and landed in Victoria, whilst climbing to eight thousand five hundred feet to get over the mountains and fly past the highest peak of Mount Kosciuszko, which stands 7,310 feet above sea level.

Phillip Island

Our arrival time at Phillip Island was critical, as we had a meal booked for 5.30pm in order to be ready for the coach at 6.30pm for the drive to see the fairy penguins come ashore at dusk. Fairy penguins are small little guys living around the coasts of New Zealand and the south coast of Australia. They stand 12 inches tall (or 30 cm in Euro money) and it was amusing to hear the guides trying to persuade us to call them 'little penguins', but we ignored the whiff of political correctness and preferred the more loveable 'fairy penguin' name.

The 'Penguin Parade', as it is called, has become irritatingly commercialised, with two gift shops selling tacky stuffed penguin toys, fast food restaurants of the charm-challenged plastic variety, and a photo booth where you can have your photo taken petting a computer-generated penguin. How tacky is that? The revenue for this venture is, apparently, totally unconnected with the 'No Photography' rule for the real penguins. Having said all that, the fairy penguins rise above the blatant money-spinning activities and steal the show. We sat on wooden benches overlooking the wide beach down to the sea shore, waiting for dusk to fall and straining our eyes for black blobs floating on the water.

Gradually, a black floating raft of penguins reaches the shoreline and, it seems as one, pop up into the standing position at the water's edge. We see more groups of thirty to forty tiny penguins, with their prominent white shirt fronts, gathering and hopping from foot to foot in a clear state of anxious expectation. Gradually, a penguin out of one group feels sufficiently brave to set off across the open beach crossing, where he will be vulnerable to fox or sea eagle predators. His courage is rubbed off on the other members of his group and the charge begins, with the first wave doing their waddling run, leaning forward and waving their short wings until the safety of the dunes is reached, where they stop for a well-earned breather. We were seated in pole position, just feet away from this rest haven, and could only look lovingly at these cute little creatures. Over the next thirty minutes or so, wave after wave made the perilous journey, occasionally with a few false starts and a regroup until sufficient collective courage was found.

Gradually, as their breath was recovered, they wandered off in ones and twos, looking like miniature waiters searching for their customers. They were setting off on the long walk to their burrows, scattered around the dunes, where they regurgitate their day's fishing catch to their families. The babies need to build their strength, for at the tender age of ten weeks they go to sea and may stay at sea for up to two years before returning home to find their mate and, hopefully, a beachfront property in the dunes.

Melbourne

After breakfast on the Monday, we took off from runway 22 on the gravel airstrip on Phillip Island. It would be only a short flight of half an hour to Melbourne. After take off we made a small diversion to fly over the motor racing circuit so Paul could take some photos, then back over French Island and across Port Phillip Bay. Not having been to Melbourne and having heard so many good things

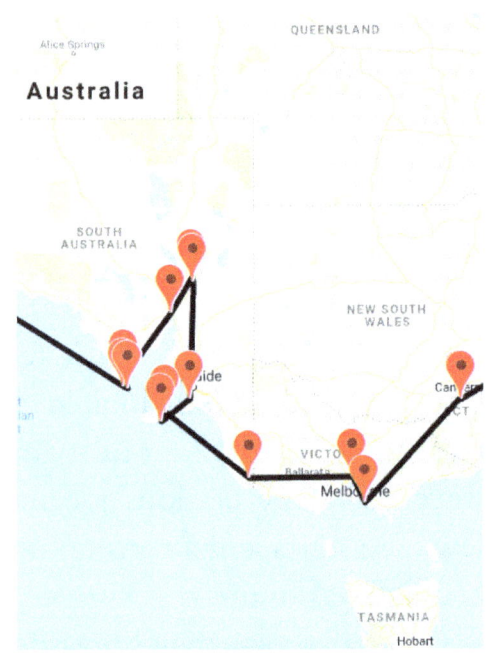

about the city, I was looking forward to the visit. We were to land at Essendon Airfield, which has been replaced by the newer Melbourne International Airport located only five miles away, to the north west. As we crossed the Yarra River we found our route taking us surprisingly close to the skyscrapers of Melbourne City. The commercial jets fly an almost parallel approach, just three miles to the east of our flight path.

After lunch, Paul and I took the tram to the impressive yellow and red brick building of Flinders Street Railway

Station. We decided to take the city tour on an historic tram car, which takes about an hour, on a squarish route around the docks and the city. The city tour is also free, a point not lost upon my Yorkshire companion. The tram made a ten minute stop at the Parliament House building, of European design with white stone, Roman columns, carved stone relief panels, and attractive black and gold wrought iron lamp posts with multi-branched arms holding white glass lamp globes, surmounted by a gold crown, that would not have been out of place in front of the Palacio Real in Madrid.

In keeping with a theme of many of my trips, I failed to resist buying another hat! This time I have added an akubra to my collection, which I thought gave me a dashing air, but this was not a universally

shared opinion. We topped the day off with a delicious steak meal at The Point restaurant, overlooking Albert Park Lake.

Kangaroo Island

We had a long day's flying ahead of us so met for an early briefing for our journey to Kangaroo Island, just off the coast from Adelaide. The route was mainly coastline past Torquay and Anglesea, then, after rounding Cape Otway, along the coast of Victoria, made famous for its twelve apostle rocks stranded in the sea, which had been separated from the coastal cliffs by the waves of the Southern Ocean. We passed by more British town names, Peterborough and Portland, mixed in with Aboriginal names, Geelong and Warrnambool, then over the gaily named Port Fairy, which I hope they do not rebrand as Port Little. Our refuelling and lunch stop was at Mount Gambier, where we needed to put our watches back half an hour to give the local time.

With a further two hours of flying to go to Kangaroo Island, Paul took over the left-hand seat, with me assuming the undemanding role as navigator and radio operator. We flew over Lake Albert and alongside the surprisingly small mouth of Australia's longest river, the Murray River. The coastline changed from steep yellow and orange cliffs to rolling green rocks, cleaved with sandy inlet coves, curving gently into the sea. We left the mainland just south of Adelaide to fly across the delightfully named Backstairs Passage for our landing on Kangaroo Island. A photo of me in my new hat was immediately posted on the internet for the benefit of friends and family following our progress. Not sure that my enthusiasm for the headgear was very much shared, or even noticed. Audiences can be very fickle!

We had a treat in store for our evening dinner. Craig and Janet Wickham were our hosts on Kangaroo Island and we drove to their woodland home for dinner. We were met, on a woodland path, by Craig, who casually pointed to the top of a slender eucalyptus tree, where a koala bear sat munching his leafy meal. An everyday sight for Craig but we all got a bit excited. Our hosts had cooked a succulent lamb dish in their outdoor brick-built pizza oven, served with roasted orange kumar potatoes and green beans. We had, luckily, stopped at the bottle shop on the way so did not run out of red wine from the Barossa Valley.

Our schedule included a full day on the island. We were met in the morning by Rob, one of Craig's guides, for an island tour in his air-conditioned coach. The island was bigger than we expected, ninety-three miles in length and thirty-five miles wide. We were staying in Kingscote and our first port of call was Seal Bay, nearly forty miles away. On the way, we passed the house of Rob's great great grandmother, built in the mid-1880s. We stopped for a photo of the oldest tree on the island, a Mulberry tree, believed to have been planted in 1836 by Dick's great great grandfather, Carl Friedrich Kleemann, who had emigrated to Australia from Germany. Dick thinks Carl came from Hamelin in Northern Germany, famous for the tale of the Pied Piper. Photos were taken of Dick standing proudly alongside 'his' tree.

Dick related how, when the ship carrying the settlers was one day out from Kangaroo Island, Carl's wife sadly died, leaving ten motherless children. The next day, Carl wisely married his children's nanny and a practical solution was found to the needs of everyone. The settlers' stay on Kangaroo Island was short, as the shortage of water did not favour farming of the land. The German settlers moved inland to the now-famous Barossa Valley, where the German culture can still be found among the vineyards and towns.

As we continued on our journey, Rob related how the island got its name. The island was discovered by the explorer Matthew Flinders in 1802. It is fair to say that the indigenous Aborigines knew about the island and had lived on it some two thousand years ago, before returning to the mainland. Captain Flinders was sailing around South Australia in HMS Investigator, but his crew were suffering badly from a lack of fresh meat. Hunting parties sent ashore to the mainland were having little success in catching the many kangaroos, as they had learned to be wary of humans, having been hunted by Aborigines. With his crew suffering poor health and some close to death, Flinders spotted the island, with thousands of kangaroos that were unaware of the dangers posed by man. The ship was restocked with fresh meat and, in honour of the animal that saved the lives of his men, Flinders named it Kangaroo Island.

Seal Bay is home to Australian sea lions, who return to it every night. They sit on the beach in family groups and we were able to walk on the beach and observe and photograph them at close quarters. One or two young males made half-hearted attempts to challenge the large dominant male with his grey fur mane, but they were quickly rebuffed in their

unsuccessful coup, an attempt to take control of his many wives and pups. This was the only remaining colony of sea lions on the island, as the others had been wiped out by the visiting American seal hunters in the 1800s. The bay was well-protected by a reef that prevented boats from entering.

From Seal Bay we drove onto the Flinders Chase National Park, which we were informed is the same size as Singapore, which will be useful information for when I finally get to visit Singapore. Fire is an essential regenerative process for the vegetation in the park. Lightning strikes are attracted by the ironstone soil, causing fires during the storms. Dormant seed pods burst open with the heat, germination is stimulated, the ash provides nutrients, and new plant life begins. Unfortunately, nature overdid things in 2007, when 98% of the national park was burned down. Yet five years later there is virtually no sign of this destructive event, and the trees and bushes burst with healthy growth.

Our lunch today was a barbecue under a copse of sugar gum trees. A little unsettling, as these trees are known as the 'Widow Maker' due to their propensity to drop limbs as a result of termites hollowing out a nest at the point a large branch joins the main tree trunk. Rob seemed relaxed, so we followed his lead and started on the cool white wine as he grilled King George whiting, potatoes, and halloumi cheese, which with the salad made a delicious al fresco meal complemented by a bottle or two (not each!) of False Cape Sauvignon Blanc, produced on one of the Kangaroo Island vineyards.

Suitably mellowed, we drove next to the Remarkable Rocks, which did indeed live up to their name. The rocks are an outcrop cluster of large granite boulders that have been worn by the wind and rain into fascinating shapes worthy of any sculptor of abstract form. The rocks also have orange lichen growing on them that adds to their visual attraction. We had fun exploring the surreal hollows and artistic forms of the rocks, crawling in the tunnels through the rocks, as well as trying the hollowed-out armchair shapes, all the while enjoying the views out to sea.

Cape du Couedic, named after a French Sea captain, is at the rocky south western point of the island and it was no surprise that a lighthouse was situated here. We descended the wooden steps and boardwalk viewpoints until we were just above the level of the sea to admire and photograph the New Zealand fur seals basking on the rocks. Rob was a mine of fascinating information and asked us why we thought lighthouses were built as high towers. The obvious answer was to extend the horizon range of the beam, which was certainly true, but Rob had an additional explanation. Before the availability of engine power, lighthouse keepers needed a way to rotate the large lens assembly, allowing the beam to sweep the sea it was protecting. This was achieved by the lighthouse keeper winding a weight to the top of the lighthouse and, as this sunk slowly under the force of gravity, the rope to which it was attached operated the clockwork gear mechanism to rotate the lens assembly. Several hours later, one hopes four or more, the lighthouse keeper was once again winding the weight back up to the top. The introduction of engine power could probably be correlated with the reduction in the girth of lighthouse keepers' biceps.

A fascinating day topped off with my first sighting of a wild echidna, amongst many other protected animals on a delightful island and environmental sanctuary.

Wilpena Pound

I had never heard of Wilpena Pound. Was it an Australian poet? Perhaps an animal reservation? Or even a new currency to replace the Australian dollar? I was told that I was not alone in my confusion as many Australians did not know of its existence either.

But first we had to get there – wherever 'there' might be. Our first concern was fuel, as there was no Avgas facility on the island, so we made a short flight to the mainland, landing at Aldinga just south of Adelaide to refuel. Aldinga was home to the Adelaide Biplanes Club, with wonderful facilities in which to enjoy coffee and home-made Anzac biscuits.

Returning to the air, we flew over a town called Clare, which our tour leader had modestly forgotten to mention was named after him. We were now flying past the Barossa Valley vineyards and climbing to six thousand five hundred feet as the land rose gently beneath us. Wilpena Pound turned out to be a vast crater, a natural amphitheatre of mountains in the Flinders Ranges National Park. Captain Matthew Flinders RN (1774 - 1814) certainly left his mark around these parts, but he did share out the glory by naming the channel between the mainland and Tasmania, Bass Straits, after his ship's surgeon. Flinders is also credited with coining the name 'Australia', to replace the two earlier names of New Holland and New South Wales.

The Electric Spark that Jumps

Our landing strip was a short dirt bush strip to one side of the crater. My first attempt at a landing saw me too high and too fast on the final approach so, applying full power, I went around for a second go that turned out to be a 'greaser', which was good fortune as Graham was taking a video of my landing.

The lodges in the park were just over a mile away, and we arrived just as the bar was opening for our traditional post-flying beer. This time we chose bottles of Beez Neez beer, which hit the spot. Dinner was kangaroo starter with a main course of rack of lamb accompanied by red wine 'du region', of course, before settling down for the night in our comfortable woodland cabins.

We enjoyed a chill-out morning relaxing and reading in this peaceful location. Daddy emu and his four chicks ambled past my cabin window, pecking at the bright orange berries on the salt bushes and eating the grass. I initially assumed it was Mummy emu but was corrected by the ranger, who explained that the male chases the female off the nest once she has laid her green eggs. He sits and incubates the eggs without leaving for food or water then brings them up single-handedly. All of which must leave a lot of time for his wife to go shopping.

After a light lunch, we met up with Michael, who was our guide on a 'Drive through Time', examining the exposed rock faces that reveal the geographical strata laid down over millions of years. Geology is one of the subjects that has eluded me and now seemed a good opportunity to learn a little more. Michael

explained that Wilpena Pound was not an extinct volcano nor the site of a meteor impact but was formed when the hard quartzite rocks were moved by the folding, lifting, and twisting of the earth's crust as the tectonic plates moved along the fault lines. The Pound is 17km long and 8km wide and is Australia's largest geological site. After this promising start, somehow all those Pre-Cambrian, Cambrian, Jurassic, Cenozoic periods etcetera became quickly merged into a geological soup in my brain, and I have to admit that my attention did begin to wander after four hours of this riveting data download.

In fairness to Michael, he did not lack enthusiasm or a sense of humour, gleaned largely from Christmas crackers.

"The ABC mountain range is so called because there are twenty-six hills, except at Christmas when there are twenty-five, as there is Noel." Boom boom!! "What was the name of swagman in Waltzing Matilda? It's Andy."

"Andy?" we question.

"Yes." Sing the song and you will see…

Once a jolly swagman camped by a billabong
Under the shade of a coolibah tree,

Andy *sang as he watched and waited till his billy boiled:*

"You'll come a-waltzing Matilda, with me."

It wasn't all rocks though, as there were trees too. Lots of trees. Pretty much all of them were red river gum eucalyptus trees, with their pale melon yellow fruit having fallen on the roadside. We spotted yellow-footed rock wallabies hidden on the cliff face, for which we needed our binoculars. The wallabies have a mustard yellow fur shirt front and four feet, plus a yellow tail with black rings around it.

The beer tasted even better that evening.

Port Lincoln

As much fun as geology is, we all agreed that flying was more fun, so next morning we took off from the dirt strip and looked at Wilpena Pound from the air. Fair to say it is impressive.

First stop was Port Augusta to refuel. Although only a forty minute flight, it was a little eventful for VH-RYB when Dick noticed that the battery charge indicator was reading zero. This normally signals that the alternator is no longer recharging the battery and it is important to conserve the available battery power and land to investigate the problem. Talking it over with Martin, they decided that by switching off all non-essential electrical systems there would be sufficient battery power to get to Port Lincoln. And that was how it worked out. On removal of the engine cowling it became clear that the fan belt was broken and the reason why the alternator was not doing its job. Due to Graham's excellent planning there was a spare fan belt in the hold, and this was fitted, although that exercise required calling upon Paul's motor engineering skills to perform the task.

Port Augusta turned out to be the regional headquarters of the Australian Royal Flying Doctor Service. Gone are the days of the black and white films we used to watch of the RFDS using old and slow bush planes designed in the 1930's (like the ones we were flying!). Nowadays, they have the sleek and fast Pilatus PC12 aircraft, fitted out like an airborne hospital ward, with two beds and medical equipment.

With all aircraft refuelled and repaired, we set off for our one and a half hour flight to the southern tip of the Eyre Peninsula, where we would be landing, at Port Lincoln. We had been advised of a NOTAM (notice to airmen) for Port Lincoln that warned of flocks of galahs in the vicinity of the airfield. The galah is a small and pretty cockatoo with a pale grey

coat and rose pink chest that can be quickly turned into a feathery mess if it flies into a propeller, with a bad result for everyone involved. Apparently galahs are edible and the recipe requires boiling the galah in water together with a rock. Once the rock is soft then the galah is ready to eat!

Port Lincoln, where we all had a galah-free landing, is home to the Australian tuna fishing fleet for the Southern Ocean. So high has been the demand for tuna from Japan that the town now boasts more millionaires per head of population than anywhere else in Australia.

The fishing fleets sail into the Southern Ocean searching for shoals of tuna. A chum boat holds the tuna in position by feeding them while the trawlers encircle the shoal with a net. Now captive, the huge net, with up to fifteen thousand tuna, is towed back to Port Lincoln at one mile per hour on a journey that can take three to six weeks. When in the Boston Bay, the tuna are transferred to static ring nets, where they are fed and fattened to the size and meat quality required by the Japanese buyers, being harvested for market some six months later.

Our journey was not to catch tuna but to swim with them. We took a boat out across Boston Bay to one of the vast ring nets in the sea, complete with a platform where we were kitted out with wet suits, masks, snorkels, rubber boots, and rubber gloves. It was explained that the gloves were essential because fingers looked very similar to pilchards in the water and tuna were happy to see if one's fingers were edible. Everyone chose to wear the rubber gloves. Suitably attired, we were invited to get in the water within the penned-off area of sea and swim with the tuna. Our tuna swimming companions were young and small at only forty to sixty kilos! Believe me, that is one big fish, and it swims beneath you like a rocket-powered, glossy steel grey missile, especially when being thrown handfuls of pilchards just where you are doing doggy paddle in the water. It was very exciting. These were blue fin tuna and while the main fins are metallic blue they have rows of tiny bright yellow fins above and below their tail section as well as a yellow stripe on their tails. The only way they get oxygen is through swimming and they never stop, day or night, so live a high speed existence.

We left the main tuna pool and transferred to a smaller fish pool to swim with snappers, mulloway, kingfish, morwong, and pilchards. Only after we got out of the smaller pool were we told that it also contained sharks! Don't worry, "they are harmless," they said. I wondered if the sharks knew that too? So one of the divers went to the floor of the pool and brought up first a toothless banjo shark and then a Port Jackson or dog shark. Hmmmm! I remained unconvinced.

Willy was fascinated by the separate rock pool with its starfish, scallops, and sea anemones. We were allowed to hold the bright orange starfish and the sea anemones, which walked with their spines on the palms of our hands, giving a tickling sensation. Willy was much amused by the fan-shaped scallop shells that, when lifted out of the water, would sit on your hand and chatter like a ventriloquist's dummy.

It was a fabulous day and that evening, in the restaurant, we even ate tuna steak! The freshest and best I have ever tasted. I should have warned the vegetarians not to read this paragraph. Ah well, it's too late now.

Nullabor Plain

I had assumed that Nullabor was an Aboriginal name. How wrong I was. I should have paid more attention in Latin classes. It comes from 'Nullus' meaning 'No' and 'Arbor', meaning 'Tree', as in 'arboretum', hence a plain with no trees. As indeed it turned out to be.

First we needed to leave the nouveau riche of Port Lincoln behind for the flight to the town of Forrest, which was pretty much in the middle of the Nullabor Plain. It did seem curious that the only town within the 77,000 square miles of this treeless terrain should be named 'Forrest'. With over five hours of flying ahead of us, a refuelling stop was required, which we took at Ceduna. For the first time on this trip we

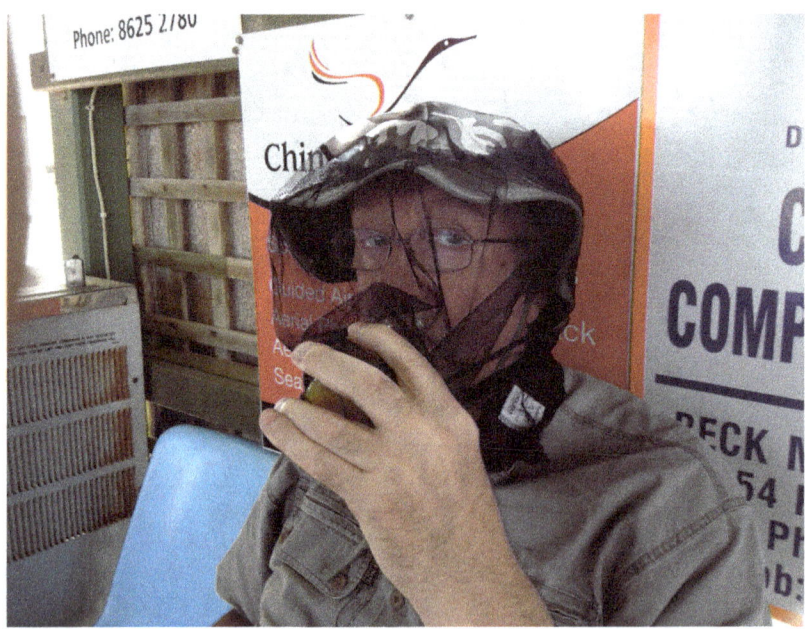

made the acquaintance of the Australian flies, which must be among the world's most persistent and invasive little beggars. Fly nets were issued to keep the flies out of our eyes and from crawling up our nostrils. Eating a picnic lunch wearing a fly net covering the whole of one's head does present its own challenges.

From Ceduna we followed the coastline of the Great Australian Bight, leaving behind the sandy beaches and inlet coves in favour of limestone cliffs striped in earth yellows, ochre reds and browns that rose to some three hundred feet above the sea. At Eucla, we turned inland for sixty-five miles over an unvarying flat landscape, with nothing but scrub bushes and definitely no water. As advised we checked the runway at Forrest for kangaroos, emus, camels, and wombats (harder to see) before landing in the hot, humid, and windy conditions. We had the luxury of hangaring our aircraft for the night, thus avoiding the chore of hammering iron spikes into the earth in order to tie them down.

The 2006 census recorded eighteen inhabitants at Forrest, but by the time we arrived there were only two left, Claas and his wife, Tania. So we met and dined with the whole town that night. Our accommodation was in bungalows, each with four bedrooms with iron bedsteads and simple and rugged décor, as befits an outback township. As we sipped our drinks on the verandah of Claas and Tania's bungalow, the only one with a fridge full of beer and wine, the sky darkened and a thunderstorm came through Forrest, with forked lightning and heavy rain, before racing away across the leaden skies.

Forrest is on the railway line from Adelaide to Perth, which has the honour of incorporating the longest stretch of straight railway line in the world, being 479 kilometres or nearly 300 miles. The area is so flat that one can see the headlight on the approaching locomotive for twenty minutes, they say, before the train passes. The station is no longer used as a passenger stop but the train does slow to deliver the mail, Tania's groceries, and collect her shopping list for the following week. The airfield was built in the late 1920's as an overnight stop for Sir Norman Brearley's West Australian Airways.

The DH66 Hercules biplane with three engines (one on the nose and one on each wing), cruising at 100mph did not have the speed or range to get from Adelaide to Perth in one flight and needed an overnight stop and refuelling station. I did like the note to passengers which reads, "The engine is not needed in landing, the plane can be landed perfectly with the engine entirely cut off. From an altitude of 2,500 feet, it is possible to glide with engine stopped, to any paddock or landing place anywhere within an area of 25 square miles". Pilots know, and practise, this, but we don't usually volunteer this information to our passengers.

Derek Alway

Albany

If yesterday had been a long flying day, today was to be even longer, with two refuelling stops. We were awakened at 5.30am for a sleepy-eyed briefing and, to make matters worse, we had forecast headwinds of between 30 and 40 knots. The first job was to get back to the coast and, I must admit, I was pleased to leave the monotonous and waterless flat terrain of the Nullabor Plain behind us. We flew at five hundred feet above the sea to our first refuelling stop at Caiguna, which turned out to be little more than a gravel strip alongside a lonely, but welcome, roadhouse on the Eyre Highway, which crosses, east to west, the 680 miles of Nullarbor Plain. Amazingly, to get to the fuel pumps we had to taxi off the runway and down a dirt path, through the bush to the back of the roadhouse. Aircraft refuelled at the back of the roadhouse and cars refuelled out the front, with little company other than the pump attendant and ten thousand over-friendly flies.

Airborne once more, we were back to battling the headwinds and three hours later we arrived at Esperance, requiring a quick turnaround to get to our destination before nightfall. Our aircraft, Charlie Echo Victor, had been very well-behaved up to now, if we don't count the time that we experimented with the autopilot and the aircraft promptly set off out to sea on a direct heading for Antarctica. We hand flew the rest of the way! But here in Esperance, our starter motor became grumpy.

The Electric Spark that Jumps

It decided that turning the engine over was too much hard work and resorted to groaning as we turned the ignition key. The plan was to let her cool down and try it again. After a few false starts she leapt into life, leaving the thought in our minds that she might not make it to Perth after all.

For this last leg into Albany the wind was in a capricious mood, and we had a very bumpy flight handling the turbulence. At one stage Paul's head hit the roof, as one sudden drop of the aircraft lifted both of us out of our seats. No better reminder needed as to why we wear seatbelts when flying. Not surprisingly, the landing at Albany was sporty, to use a euphemism, and that is not what you require after seven and a quarter hours of concentrated flying. We were more than ready for our post-flight beer.

We were staying in a delightful boutique hotel, the Beach House at Bayside, run by retired farmers Keith and Janet and their daughter Sally. Keith and Janet cooked a wonderful meal of roast lamb and fresh vegetables, followed by local cheeses and fine red wine. After such a long and tiring day it was little wonder that I slept solidly for ten hours that night.

We had a rest day on Tuesday and it was most welcome. A lazy breakfast of healthy fruit was followed by an unhealthy breakfast of bacon, eggs, mushrooms, and tomato, with as much toast as we could eat. Delicious. The breakfast was also memorable for

Martin's decision to ignore the written instructions on the toaster and extend the cook time for his bread, resulting in the smoke alarm incident that he never lived down. Toaster licence withdrawn pending further training!

Clare had organised a tour of the town and its surroundings. Albany is a port town on the northern shore of the Princess Royal Harbour, linked to the King George Sound by the very narrow Ataturk Channel. The name for this channel comes from its association with the Anzac troop ships leaving for Gallipoli during the First World War and the reconciliatory donations from the President of Turkey, Mustafa Kemal Atatürk, towards the cost of building the war memorial.

Our driver took us first to the war memorial on a hill overlooking the harbour, King George Sound, and the islands of Michaelmas and Breaksea. The memorial is approached through an avenue of 122 trees, each with a plaque bearing the name of an Albany soldier lost in the First World War. Atop the memorial plinth is a bronze statue of a soldier with two Brumby horses, commemorating the Australia and New Zealand Mounted Division, formed in Egypt in 1916 and seeing service in the Middle East and fighting in the Sinai and Palestine Campaigns.

The coastline is rocky and this, mixed with the gale force winds, produces great waves that crash against the granite rocks, emitting tall plumes of sea water spray at the narrow cut inlet and under the Rock Bridge. A Dutch captain, François Thijssen, in his ship, the Gulden Zeepaert (or Golden Seahorse), was the first to explore this coast, amazingly in 1627. For the next two hundred years there were expeditionary visits by the French and British, including our old friend Captain Matthew Flinders, until 1826, when a British Army expedition led by Major Edmund Lockyer arrived on the Amity, established a garrison, and later claimed Albany for the British.

Albany, named after one of the sons of King George III, was Australia's last whaling station until 1978, when all whaling was banned in Australia. In fact it was part of the purpose of Major Lockyer's garrison to protect the whalers from marauding French warships. Indeed, later, the Amity was to become a whaling ship. The main purpose of whaling in the 1800s was to extract whale oil. Before the availability of refined oils, whale oil was used to power the world's oil lamps. Whale oil was also required by the food and cosmetics industries, the latter also taking the ambergris from the digestive system and spermaceti found in the head cavities of the whale. Little went to waste, with the baleen hair, found in the whale's mouth for filtering out krill, being used as whalebones, allowing seductive corsetry to be tightly laced to secure the nipped-in waist look that weakens men's knees – well my knees at least!

Work on a whaling station was undoubtedly a very tough life, with work beginning at 4.30am each day and only ending when the work was complete. It mattered not that one might only complete the day's work at midnight, one was still required to be back at 4.30am for the next day. It was dangerous and physically demanding work in these large scale abattoirs, but a flenser, whose job it was to remove the outer layer of blubber using a long-handled axe, would always get a seat in the pub, being oblivious of the stench exuding from his skin. Over the many years of hunting first the humpback and later the sperm whales, Albany whaling station caught and processed over 25,000 of these magnificent creatures. Now, except for the intransigence of the Japanese whalers, it is largely a thing of the past, and stocks of these ocean leviathans are returning to those of former glory years.

Wednesday the 4th of August was due to be the day when we turned north, leaving the Southern Ocean for the Indian Ocean on the West coast of Australia, but the weather had other ideas. No flying was possible, as a cold frontal system worked its way past the south west corner of Australia. Hopes for an improvement in the afternoon, when a blue sliver was spotted overhead, proved to be unfounded optimism, so we spent the day looking at the cloudy sky, sampling the beers, and generally lazing about. Dick, Graham, and Clare managed to get a hot tub working so sipped their beers whilst soaking their naked bodies in a room heavy with steam. Probably best to leave that story there – least said, soonest mended.

Busselton

As soon as we awoke on Thursday morning, the curtains were drawn apart to find the sky was full of blue patches, enough to make a dozen shirts, among the high and scattered cumulus and the occasional stormy squall racing across the sky. Clearly it was flyable but it would be 'oh so' windy. So we decamped to the airfield, refuelled, and waited for a big blue patch that allowed us to fly through the hole in the clouds and be on our way.

I don't think I will ever forget the look of surprise on Paul's face that day. For the leg from Albany to Busselton it was Paul's turn to fly as pilot in command. Not only was the wind strong but it was also gusting. After completing the pre-take off checks and confirming the compass was aligned on our runway heading, Paul advanced the throttle lever to full power and we began gathering speed on our take off run, waiting for the rotate speed of 55 knots, the minimum velocity to get our baby into the air. Unfortunately, we had only reached 40 knots when a huge gust of wind came at us straight down the runway and we were airborne.

Now, both Paul and I knew that our plane does not fly at 40 knots in still air, and the wind was throwing our aircraft around like an autumn leaf in a gale. With both hands gripping the control column tightly, we slid and slewed from side to side while climbing, at rather less than the recommended smooth trajectory, in the turbulent air as we gradually vectored our craft away from the coastal weather that was giving us all this grief. Forgotten were all the good airmanship and airfield practices of flying down the runway centre line, this was survival first and good practices second. An hour and a half later, somewhat bumped and bruised but in one piece, we completed our inland track and arrived at a calmer Busselton on the shores of Geographe Bay.

We were met by our charming white-haired lady guide and driver, Pat, for a tour of the Margaret River wineries and breweries. We didn't let the wineries down, with our enthusiastic sampling of the Semillon Sauvignon Blancs or 'SSB' as the Aussies abbreviate it. Pat took us to a brewery that, in its estate, had a large lake featuring a tall blue metal girder rising, at a forward angle, out of a flowerhead fountain with a glamourous golden statue of a shapely young woman mounted on the top as she prepares to dive gracefully into the water below. Australians, with their preference for the prosaic over the eloquence of language, have named her the 'Chick on a Stick'. It does, however, reflect their wry and earthy sense of humour, delivered with minimum effort. It must be the hot climate!

With the 'Chick' still in our minds we set about sampling the various beers on the five-beer taster palette

The Electric Spark that Jumps

– one palette each that is. This all descended into a student-style speed drinking competition that, interestingly, Clare won hands down. Funny what one finds out about people on a three week trip together! Life was starting to take on a foggy glow, not helped by

ensuring that, at the next stop, we validated the claims of the viticulturist that the 2009 cabernet merlot blend was his finest vintage.

The Last Leg

It was Friday, 6th April, and we had just one more leg to fly to reach our goal of arriving in Perth. It was a short one hour flight, landing at Jandakot and parking up outside the Royal Aero Club. For Martin, Barbara and Willy this was the end of their adventure in Australia, as it was for Paul and me. Dick would fly Romeo Yankee Bravo back to Toowoomba, taking a mostly direct route, enjoying the company of a couple of old airline mates. Charlie Echo Victor needed a new starter motor fitted then would be taken over by friends from the earlier

Canada safari, Ian Buchan and his daughter Fiona, who were undertaking the northern route back to Brisbane.

So after seventy-nine hours and twelve minutes of flying, Paul and I had 'Closed the Loop' by completing our circumnavigation of Australia, albeit with a six and a half year break in the middle. It had been a fantastic adventure full of great memories and new friends.

Derek Alway

Footnote

I did not write a journal for the 2005 trip around the Northern half of Australia but I did write some light-hearted doggerel which I include below for, I hope, your amusement.

Ode to a GOANA Experience
Shepherd of the Aussie skies
Goatee beard and steely eyes
Captain Keith tending his flock
Skyhawks all with throttle lock
There's Gordon nursing Shirley's back
Brian and Sharon dressed in black
Bill and Sherry from Oregon State
Keith and Rhonda call us "mate"
Paul is such a Yorkshire lad
Derek is an English cad
Aussie skies flown with finesse
Navigation GPS!
Perth, Carnarvon, Coral Bay
Tracking north we find the way
Swinging slowly to the east
Port Hedland and at Broome we feast
Broome to Derby, say it right
It's getting hot, a sticky night
Early start and inland farther
Hostile terrain to Kununarra
Feeding wallabies water melon
Then our laurels not to rest on
Cruise the Ord spotting crocs
Counting 'freshie' and 'saltie' stocks
Flying through the outback smoke
The turbulence is no joke
Overflying Tipperary

Derek Alway

Cooinda landing is quite scary
Boating on the Yellow river
Big croc, Pluto, makes us shiver
The jabiru in reeds does wallow
Catches snake, we watch it swallow
Flight to Burketown long and hot
Outback lodgings – that's our lot
Bore hole water steams from ground
Scores of wallabies around
Gold rush town, Charters Towers
Flocks of fruit bats in the bowers
Ghosts of miners in the air
Nineteenth century buildings there
Large mag drop delays our start
Keith calmly takes engine apart
Flight test first then all away
Up in the blue and sunny day
Whitsundays sighted amid sighs
Brampton Island paradise
Dining under palms and stars
Southern Cross, Venus and Mars
Snorkelling and island walks
Then time for one of Keith's talks
Redcliffe is our destination
Pilots make your preparation
Check the fuel and oil each day
Clean windshield, wipe bugs away
Rolling mag checks, note the time

The Electric Spark that Jumps

Apply full power start the climb
This has been a wondrous trip
Thanks to Keith's fine leadership
You've kept us safe, feasted our eyes
Captain of the Aussie skies.

The Day We Went to Bantry

Ireland from 26 May to 3 June 2013

G-BOFA
Derek Alway
Martin McClelland

G-DAKO
Paul Edwards
Nick Snaith

The Day We Went to Bantry

We had to get this landing right first time. Bantry Airfield is a small earlobe of flat land stuck on the side of the banks of Bantry Bay. There is a tarmac landing strip that is only 450 metres in length, with an approach over water and the touchdown point starting after a thin strip of pebble beach. It is important to stop before the end of the runway, as that becomes Bantry Bay again, very quickly, with little room for options.

This called for our best short field landing technique, which we practise, but on longer runways such as our 750m runway at Denham, which allows escape options when we don't get it just right. The trick is to get your approach speeds spot on.

On the downwind leg, when we flew parallel to the runway in the opposite direction of our landing, we had to avoid exceeding eighty knots. Turning onto base leg and descending from one thousand feet to five hundred feet over the water, we slowed to seventy knots before aligning on the runway heading and reducing our airspeed to sixty-five knots. It was all a matter of flying slowly enough to land and brake in three hundred metres while slowing the airspeed to a thin margin of safety above the stall speed – when the lift from the air would no longer support the aircraft. Get it wrong and three hundred metres becomes five hundred very quickly.

It helps when there is a headwind and, that day, we were lucky to have fifteen knots straight down the runway. This meant that our airspeed of sixty-five knots became fifty knots over the ground, making the pilot's job that much easier. Then we pulled back the power over the pebble strip of beach, slowing to sixty knots, flared gently while the wheels kissed the numbers at the start of the runway, and we'd made it. One or two, with less experience, have not been so lucky and tasted the water at the other end of this minute airfield.

But I am getting ahead of myself.

The Electric Spark that Jumps

We were on a nine day flying trip around Ireland. Each year the Denham Flying Group organises a summer trip and this year we were 'doing Ireland'. We were meant to be five aircraft, but BIBA had a mechanical problem and the Tango Tango crew expressed concern over the weather forecast for our chosen week in Ireland. So it was just Paul and Nick in DAKO and Derek and Martin in BOPA as the 'synchro pair', with Rex and Richard in BUFY out there somewhere, doing their own thing.

The weather was rubbish on the Friday, a bit better on Saturday but, with the promise of a brief spell of good weather for the bank holiday weekend, we planned to depart on Sunday 26 May. We filed our paperwork to satisfy the requirements of Customs, Border Force, Special Branch and Air Traffic Control, for a departure around midday. BOPA left from Denham and DAKO left from Durham Teeside, as Paul had swung by to check on his mum on Saturday afternoon. We flew to Weston, which is the private flight airfield for Dublin. We had to follow a prescribed routing to avoid the main commercial flights airport of Dublin by flying to the Pigeon House Chimneys, easy to spot as they are painted in red and white stripes, before turning west to follow the river Liffey into Weston. What the charts do not tell you is that the Liffey is so narrow that it can be quite hard to spot between the houses along its banks. It is said that one of the bridges over the Liffey is wider than it is long!

The charts did warn one to stay clear of the military airfield of Baldonnel Casement, which is surprisingly close by. I was navigating that day and when given clearance for a straight in on runway 25 at Weston I advised my pilot, Martin, to come right thirty degrees.

"No need," said Martin, "I am lined up on finals now."

I was just wondering why the small airfield of Weston had more runway lights than Heathrow when our headsets were filled with the voice of an air traffic controller demanding an immediate turn right of thirty degrees to avoid entering the restricted airspace of Baldonnel!! Poor Martin did not live this down for quite some time. We all knew that it was an easy mistake to make, that we had made our own fair share too, but friends love to tease each other mercilessly. We later discovered that not only had many other pilots made the same navigational error, but military pilots from Baldonnel had also landed at Weston by mistake!

We stayed in Dublin that night in rooms above O'Shea's Merchant pub, which, in the evening, resonated with live music. We were not far from the Temple Bar district, where people throng for the buzz, food, bars, and live music bursting out of every doorway, as well as on the streets. We ate well at The Old Storehouse, where Nathalie and Stella looked after us with excellent service and amusing banter or 'craic', as the Irish say. Slowly, we made our way back to

O'Shea's, where the music was in full swing. The first group had a young man whose dexterity on the mandolin was reminiscent of the Bluegrass music from

Tennessee. After a distracting visit to 'the Oldest Pub in Ireland', or so they claimed, for a Guinness or two and some Bushmills 21-year single malt whiskey, we returned to O'Shea's, where there was a young, blonde-haired fiddler girl playing traditional Irish music at breakneck speed while banging the boot of her left leg on the wooden floor to provide a percussive beat. We all voted her the top musician of the evening in spite of the fact that she was the prettiest by far – which goes to show how objective and unbiased we could be in our patronage.

Over an Irish Whiskey, or two, Nick encouraged us to play confession for our flying bloopers. Paul generously volunteered one of mine when, asking to turn my aircraft in a semi-circle to reverse back up the runway, I requested, "A 360 backtrack!". "Be my guest," came the reply from the tower, looking forward to enjoying my pirouette!

Then, would you believe it, Paul came up with another of my mistakes! This was the occasion when I called the tower at Kirkwall in the Orkney Islands to advise "Papa Alpha at one thousand feet and requests frequency change en-route." I received the reply, "Papa Alpha, clear for take-off!" as I had neglected to ask for, or receive, permission to depart the runway!

We all laughed over Alan's flight when he landed at Wellesbourne whilst talking on the radio to Turweston. Wellesbourne were surprised to see Alan and Turweston were left wondering where he had gone. Alan has a long explanation of this event that just fails to ring true! Nick won the confession prize, with his landing at Duxford, which has two parallel runways. When asked whether he preferred the grass runway or the tarmac runway, Nick asked, "Which one is the cheapest?"!! Come to think of it, Paul never did admit to a blooper.

After breakfast on Monday we made our way to the Guinness Museum for the tour and free glass of the black stuff with the creamy white top, apart from the pilot for the day, for whom orange juice was the vegetarian option. Arthur Guinness was clearly a man of vision and some formidable negotiating ability when he secured the Dublin land for his factory in 1759 on a 9,000 year lease for £45 per annum. No, this is not a misprint, it really is for 9,000 years. Now there was a man with a plan.

For our flight after lunch we opted for the Lambay Transit, which takes one across the water of Dublin Bay, with the air traffic requirement of 'Not above 500 feet', while the big commercial jets flew over our heads for a landing on the westerly runway at Dublin Airport. Our destination was Enniskillen, beside Lower Lough Erne, in Northern Ireland. Noel, the air traffic controller at Enniskillen, was very welcoming on the radio but said he had no idea we were coming in. We explained that we had filed flight plans. Noel then said, "Well I never received copies of your flight plans, but not to bother, and I have closed both your flight plans for you." Only in Ireland could you close flight plans you have not received!

One of the many pleasures while flying around Ireland is that with short flights each day one has time to look around and enjoy the places visited. The Manor House Country Hotel overlooked the banks of Lower Lough Erne and we decided to take advantage of its nine hole golf course after breakfast. The DAKO crew challenged the BOPA crew to a match with our rented clubs, of dubious parentage, and dress-code-offending attire. The Irish need all the money they can get right now so there

were no murmurs of dissent to be heard. The DAKO boys started off well and Nick turned out to be a demon putter from any angle and any distance. But class came through, as Martin and I knew it would, and the upstarts were soundly trounced by three holes up with two to play.

The day's flights were a trip to Donegal, back in the Republic of Ireland, after which we would return to Northern Ireland for a landing in Belfast. Each time one travels across the country border there is a requirement to file a general aviation report to customs and the police. Twelve hours' notice is required each time, but the Irish have a way of dealing with this. They first advise you of the twelve-hour statutory requirement with a straight face and then with a twinkle in the eye say, "but an hour will do, now!" Rules were not invented by the Irish and they certainly have no intention of letting anyone else's spoil their fun.

You cannot fly over the Irish countryside and fail to be impressed. This is not called 'The Emerald Isle' without reason, as it bursts with a hundred shades of green and, at this time of year, is spotted with golden yellow bursts of gorse blossom.

After a toasted sandwich lunch at Donegal, we let DAKO take off first because it is a faster aircraft and, that way, we would avoid overtaking problems. Paul decided to use the Donegal runway to practise his short field take-off technique. Now the wisdom amongst pilots is that the runway behind you is of no use, which is why we taxi all the way to the end of the runway even though we take-off well before the halfway mark. Today Paul decided to go from the halfway point on the runway – most unlike cautious Paul. Even with DAKO's powerful engine, the end of the runway appeared rather too soon so Paul employed the 'yank two stages of flap on' technique which made DAKO jump up into the air like a champagne cork, barely clearing the instrument landing sensors at the runway's end! Ha! We have his blooper on record now.

We flew along the Northern Irish coastline, past the Royal Portrush golf course, before flying low to spot the Giant's Causeway just along from Portballintrae. Later that evening, Martin would tell us the folklore behind

the Giant's Causeway, which I will retell for those who are not familiar with the story.

Once upon a time (it has to start like this of course) there was an Irish Giant by the name of Finn MacCool (or Fionn mac Cumhail in Irish; they've always been terrible spellers). There was a Scottish giant by the name of Fingal, and after some preliminary name-calling the two giants took to throwing huge rocks at each other until there was a rock path, or causeway, between Ireland and Scotland. Now Fingal was a larger giant than Finn MacCool and so Finn, being aware that the Scottish Giant could cross the causeway, needed a plan to thwart the larger giant. Finn decided to sit in a pram dressed as a baby. So when Fingal arrived in Ireland looking for a showdown, he spotted the baby and, reasoning that the 'father' must be truly enormous, ran back to Scotland, destroying the causeway as he went and then hiding in a cave, on the Isle of Staffa, now known as Fingal's Cave.

Of the three airfields in Belfast, we chose to land at Newtonards, as it was the cheapest and friendliest. Rex and Richard came to the same conclusion, having landed in BUFY ahead of us. Newtonards sits at the top of Strangford Lough and is overlooked by Scrabo Tower on the hill that rises above the adjacent approach path for the airfield. The tower was built as a memorial to one of the Duke of Wellington's generals, Charles Stewart, the 3rd Marquis of Londonderry. A golf course sits on the hilltop above the Newtonards runways. The famous

Irish golfer, Christie O'Connor, once remarked that it was the only golf course where the planes fly below you!

Belfast was the shipyard that built the Titanic, so a visit to the museum, with photos of workmen from a bygone era, was a must. I knew the ship was big but had no concept of how big until I saw the scale of the yards and the giant single gantry crane which actually straddled two parallel berths for the Titanic and her sister ship, the Olympic. Nick surprised us all with his knowledge of cranes derived from the proper job he'd had as a crane salesman. Why he packed that job in to become a DJ is beyond me.

The weather continued to be warm and sunny with high fluffy clouds as we prepared for the next day's flight to Sligo. The fields looked even greener today, edged with dark bottle green hedges or stone walls built with gaps between the stones to allow the strong westerly winds to blow through the walls rather than blow them over. The fields were numerous and mainly small in a seemingly endless variety of odd geometric shapes.

Leaving Sligo for Galway, we decided upon a coastline route to enjoy the scenery in the early evening light. Our plan was thwarted by a radio call asking if we knew that Galway Airfield closed at 5pm! No, we did not, but decided to defer the visual splendours for later as right now our priority was a parking place for the aircraft and a bed for the night for ourselves. We arrived eight minutes late and the genial fire crew waited for us.

Galway Airport is a victim of over-ambition, the bubble bursting and ensuing recession. The airport expanded to international air traffic requirements and had just completed a €5 million hangar for the Aer Arann fleet when the airline went into administration. Aer Arann withdrew its flights and Galway was left holding the €5 million debt and no international flights.

We parked next to BUFY and phoned to find out where Rex and Richard were staying so we could all have dinner together. We chose Martine's restaurant near the bottom of Quay Street and what an excellent choice it was. When you next go to Galway this is a must visit location. Excellent food, warm and cosy decor and Martine makes you feel that you are the only guests in the dining room of her house. We all agreed not to embarrass Rex by mentioning that he fell asleep while sitting up at the dinner table. I am only telling you because I know you can keep a secret.

We were a little excited over breakfast on Thursday as we discussed our plans to visit the Aran Isles. The Scottish have their own Isle of Arran in the Firth of Clyde but with a different spelling, probably because they roll their "r's" much more than the Irish. Ireland has three Aran Islands which are famous for the warm woollen sweaters, or Ganseys, with raised cable stitch design. Mark you, the Atlantic Sea off the coast of Ireland would be too cold to survive through winter without a stock of warm and weatherproof jumpers.

The Electric Spark that Jumps

We flew along the southern edge of Galway Bay and turned out to sea for the first island of Inisheer, where we practised our short field landing technique by touching our wheels down onto the tarmac runway, raising the flaps on the run, and powering away for an immediate take-off. We call that a 'touch and go' – it's what it says on the tin.

On to Inishmaan, where the runway is twenty-five metres longer, at 546 metres, for a second touch and go. We were having fun. Martin had now made two spot-on short field approaches, so time for the real thing and a landing on the 500 metre runway at Inishmore, where the islanders had thoughtfully laid a thirty yard overrun at either end. But neither pilots for the day, Martin or Paul in the heavier 235 horsepower Piper, needed the

overrun, as we landed one after the other just in front of the Aer Arann Islander twin delivering ten visitors for a day out on the island.

We took the minibus into town for tea and cake overlooking the harbour. Cycling round the island seemed to be very popular, with wave after wave of tourists on hired bikes squeezing by us on the narrow roads. Nearly bought an Aran sweater, but the shop seemed to be run by public sector employees who, the moment we started looking at their attractive knitwear announced, "shop closing now for our lunch break!". Private enterprise is not much alive or well in Inishmore.

It is difficult to overdose on coastal views from the air, especially when it is a clear day in Ireland and the shoreline has been artistically weathered and carved by

the elements. So we decided on an airborne meandering across the estuary of the River Shannon, around the Dingle peninsula, the Ring of Kerry and then into Kerry Airfield. Before we even got to Tralee, the cloud over the sea began to lower and we decided to make a run for the hills while we still had good visibility. The airfield came up a bit earlier than Martin expected and, not wishing to go-around, my intrepid pilot chose an approach path that exchanged the usual three degree glide path for one closer to sixty degrees! It worked, but the flare before touchdown was a tad sharpish. Our welcome at Kerry was unusual for the fact that we were taken into the visiting Pilots' Room and served champagne and fresh strawberries. Let's hope this is a custom that might catch on. The more observant among us, from which I excuse myself, remarked that this was to soften the blow for being charged €3 per litre for Avgas which, after all, is just leaded petrol with a fancy name.

Having arrived early we hired a car and drove around the Dingle Peninsula, stopping for tea and cakes near the harbour. At one stage we passed a shrine with religious figures in bright white stone, which prompted memories from Martin's childhood in Belfast as he unconsciously recited the chant he and his mates made while playing: "Holy Mary mother of God, chuck us down a couple of bob". It wouldn't work today, for the shilling, nicknamed a 'bob', ceased circulation after decimalisation in 1971. Was I born then? 'Fraid so. Was Nick born then? Probably not!

Friday morning was our only time during the whole week when we could not fly visually. So we had a late and long breakfast. The clouds lifted enough to fly directly to Cork but for the second time we were thwarted in our plan to fly around the Ring of Kerry.

Saturday broke with blue skies and sunshine. A corking day in Cork? Maybe, but certainly a great day to fly. And today was the day we decided to go to Bantry. It's a short runway at 450 metres, with the added problem that if you don't stop in time you finish up in Bantry Bay, regardless of which direction you land on the 07/25 runway. Paul, quite rightly, was concerned, because DAKO is a heavier aircraft than BOPA. One needs skill to land BOPA on a short runway but, with DAKO, there is even less room for error. The key factor would be the wind and today we had good fortune, with the wind off the sea and pretty much straight down the 25 westerly runway. Paul declared the mission was a 'GO'.

We phoned the airfield and spoke to Denis, who said it would take him a short while to get to the airfield, a rather grand title for this pocket handkerchief of land. He said that he should be able to hoist the windsock and be ready for us by 1230. We were a little early departing so took a circuitous route over Kinsale then the Old Head promontory, with its challenging golf course on the very tip of this windy headland. We routed along the frayed coastline of southern Ireland, with its long ragged fingers of land stretching out to sea, rock islands with grass tablecloths and wine glass bays. Entering Bantry Bay we heard from air traffic that Denis was not yet ready for us, so we explored the far side of the bay and saw the oil rig out to sea. Then Bantry Radio sparked into life with an invitation to land.

Paul went first and got the numbers spot on, landing within 300 metres and parking on the grass beside the rusty hangar. Then it was my go and it turned out alright too. Denis, who had been filming the landings on video, greeted us as long lost friends.

"Good day to you. My name is Denis Connolly and welcome to Bantry." The welcome was reprised by his cuddly golden labrador, Jazz. "Would you be liking to visit the town?" asked Denis.

In order for five of us to squeeze into Denis' tiny hatchback, it was necessary for Jazz to travel in the rear. Denis opened to hatchback door and, reluctantly, Jazz jumped in, then after a tender kiss on her forehead, Denis gently closed the door so as not to hurt his precious companion.

We had tea, served in a huge metal teapot, which washed down the thick homely sandwiches in the cafe on the harbourside. An hour later, there was Denis, waiting in his car outside the cafe, to take us back to the airfield. We were presented with the DVD of the landings at Bantry in 2012, including a helicopter visit from the Irish President, Michael D. Higgins, or as he is affectionately known on account of his diminutive stature, 'The Chief Leprechaun'. You just have to love the Irish sense of humour and the incredible warmth of their welcome.

Then it was time for photos, with Denis clicking away so that we could all appear on his Bantry Airfield Facebook page and his 2013 compilation DVD – eighteen photos no less. We are famous!! Well, at least in Bantry Airfield. As Nick so aptly put it, "It's the people who make the places special". Denis made Bantry special for us.

Our take-offs went without a hitch using Paul's champagne cork method of leaping our aircraft into the air, and we were on our way to the grass airfield at Kilkenny.

Now it is true that looking for a grass runway in a land where nearly every field is green can be challenging. We have all spent time in similar situations, knowing that the grass airfield has to be 'just down there somewhere' but failing to identify it. Today it was Nick's turn to feel foolish and, in fairness, he was not helped by Paul's ambitious and imaginative call to air traffic that he was "visual with the field and please close our flight plan" when still eleven miles away!

As BOPA is slower than DAKO, we knew we were second to arrive at Kilkenny and expected DAKO would be just landing or even parked up beside the hangar. So you can imagine our surprise when on the downwind leg for runway 27 we spotted Nick and DAKO flying in the opposite direction! Over the radio came Nick's embarrassed call that they still had no idea where the runway was and were circling and looking hard! We told Nick that we would go ahead and land, and we would have done, except that as we were on finals we heard a radio call from a powered glider announcing that as they had their engine off would we mind if they landed first. Appreciating that gliders only have one go at landing we readily gave way and powered away for another circuit. By now, the DAKO crew had untwisted their knickers and were ahead of us again and downwind. So we did land in the correct sequence after all.

Peter, the airfield owner, turned out to have been the instructor in the glider who asked us to give way on finals. He was very happy to make us all a welcoming cup of tea. Suitably refreshed, we set off for Waterford, which was only a fifteen-minute flight, for our overnight stay.

Treacy's Hotel, pronounced 'Tracey's', has the external appearance of a boutique hotel, looking smart in black and gold paintwork. Your 'curiosity is heightened when you set out in search of your rooms through a labyrinth of corridors. It was the next morning when I walked into the breakfast room, the size of a football field, filled with half of Poland and other tourists, that I understood we had stayed the night in Doctor Who's telephone box. You know, the one that is very small on the outside but enormous, with never-ending rooms, on the inside.

Our evening dinner was at the La Bohème restaurant and turned out to be a winner. Much discussion on whether it surpassed Martine's in Galway. Martine's got my vote, as I'd been the one who found that restaurant, but Nick preferred La Bohème. Guess who found La Bohème?

Waterford airport had also suffered from the recession and the loss of Aer Arann business. The skeleton staffing at the airport has just two flights a day for four days each week. So they were pleased to see us. As we prepared to leave on Sunday morning, we were told to use the 'Crew Only' channel, where the security man asked to see our boarding cards!

"But we don't have any," we explained.

"Then you need to return to the checking in desk and get boarding cards," he replied.

So Nick volunteered to return for another chat with Lisa, who hand-wrote boarding cards for our two aircraft – and now the security man was happy. Well, almost, because he still required us to put our bags through the X-ray machine, remove phones, take loose change from our pockets, and pull off our belts before we were pronounced safe to walk onto the apron.

"You must be quite busy then," I suggested. "How many aircraft are on the apron today?"

"Oh, just your two planes, lads, and have a good flight."

You can't make this stuff up!!

Paul and Nick decided to fly straight to BallyBoy for the fly-in, whilst Martin and I decided to fly up the coast. We flew east to Wexford and turned north up the coastline. After Wicklow we asked Dublin approach if we could make the Lambay Transit across Dublin Bay. I had done it earlier in the week and now it was Martin's turn. So at four hundred feet over the water we crossed the extended centreline of Dublin's 28 runway, onto which traffic was landing. Dublin advised us of "Traffic in your three o'clock high. Traffic is a triple seven, fifteen hundred feet above passing through your overhead on finals for two eight."

It was a bit hard to miss this big bird passing over us, and I tried to remain laid back with my reply,

"Copy that and visual with the traffic"! Gosh, flying can be such fun at times.

BallyBoy Airfield had a grass strip which stood out well, as the owner, Bernard, had cut two grass edge strips to form two wide and dirty white strips on either side of the green runway. Martin did a perfect landing and we spotted a 'FOLLOW ME' quad bike ahead of us, commanded by an attractive blonde chick in cool sunglasses (how do they get into those skin-tight blue jeans?) and beckoning us to follow her. And that's just what we did as we parked BOPA in the well-trodden cow-field.

Waiting to meet us on the airfield was John McKenna, who has a house in nearby Kells and whose planned route around Ireland we had pretty much followed. Alan and Tony had flown in with Tango Tango and, of course, Paul and Nick had arrived before us.

And so we had a great day in the sun, which occasionally hid behind highish clouds. I would guess that over fifty aircraft flew in for the day. We were treated to aerobatic displays by an Extreme and a couple of performance RV kit aircraft, followed by a model aircraft Extra, which performed an aerial ballet around a model Piper Cub, then a visit from the Garda helicopter, as well as the craic between the visiting pilots. Pig roast, burgers and sausage plus salad for €5, and as much tea and coffee as you wanted.

Paul and Nick flew back on Sunday evening whilst Alan, Tony, Martin, and myself enjoyed a leisurely evening at the lovely Trim Castle Hotel. The next day we repositioned the aircraft to Weston for refuelling and clearances for Customs, Border, and Special Branch. Martin and I flew back high over the clouds at 7,500 feet, descending before the Luton zone for a safe landing back home in Denham.

A great trip and 'it was the people who made it'.

The Electric Spark that Jumps

San Luis Obispo

Opulence, Absurdity and Excitement

California
April 2013

The Electric Spark that Jumps

It was my third visit to San Luis Obispo, or rather it would have been had we got there. But that's a story for later.

My first visit was in the nineteen eighties, with Angela. We were on holiday in California and had spent time seeing the sights in San Francisco. We crossed the Golden Gate Bridge, had coffee in Sausalito, were shown round Alcatraz Prison by Corky the park ranger, had driven down the wiggly Lombard Street, ridden the Powell-Mason cable car up and down the impossibly steep hills, eaten ice-cream in Ghiardelli Square, bought a pearl on Fisherman's Wharf and had dinner at the Tonga Room in the basement of the Fairmont Hotel, where there is a lake amongst the dining tables, over which thunderstorm rain fell while the band played 'I Just Called To Say I Love You'. Did I mention that the band was on a boat floating in the middle of the lake when the heavens opened?

From San Francisco we drove south to Monterey and stayed the night in Carmel before driving the Pacific Coast Highway along the Big Sur to San Luis Obispo. We had booked a night at the famous Madonna Inn, where fantasy becomes reality, bad taste décor becomes wonderful, and everything is outrageously fun. Created by Mr. Madonna in the fifties and sixties, using rocks from his two thousand acre farmland, it has one hundred and ten individually designed and quirky rooms. Angela and I stayed in the Irish Hills room which was, unsurprisingly, green with gold touches, had a rock cave shower room and a three foot model leprechaun keeping an eye on us in the bedroom suite. The colour scheme throughout the hotel is predominantly shocking pink and gold. The dining room had deep-buttoned seating, in shocking pink leather, with a life-size golden tree in the centre, while the coffee shop featured a child-sized angel on a trapeze swing that hung from the ceiling. A trip to the men's room was a risk as the urinal was a waterfall into which one peed. Turning round in mid-flow was not recommended, as visiting menfolk would occasionally bring their wives into the room announcing, "You gotta see this, honey!"

It is now April 2013 and Susie and I are on a three week visit to California where Susie has a condominium in Rancho Santa Fe just down the road from her daughter Lisa's house. The holiday location works well as Susie can spend time with her daughter and catch up with three of her grand-daughters, Jessica, Isabelle, and Millie. The endangered male species in the house is husband Kevin, who provides entertaining conversation for me while the girls do girly talk when I join the Mabbutt family for dinner.

There are plenty of diversions around the area. Just down the road is championship golf at Torrey Pines, which is a public course run by the City of San Diego. As a single player it is easy to find a game as one checks in with the starter on arrival who, being keen to have four players on the tee, will quickly find three other golfers you can join. The only real decision is whether to play the longer South Course or the slightly shorter, but still demanding, North Course. Both courses run along the cliff tops, offering stunning views overlooking the Pacific Ocean.

As a change from playing golf, I could drive north on '5', the Santa Ana Freeway, to the Palomar Airport Road exit, and hire an aircraft from McClellan-Palomar airport in Carlsbad.

Susie and I did a lot together too, visiting Old Town San Diego, shopping at one of the many malls around the area, eating at our favourite Pacifica restaurant in Del Mar, where Thursday night is half-price wine night! This year we decided to take a few days driving north beyond Los Angeles to visit Hearst Castle at San Simeon.

We set off from Rancho Santa Fe just before midday and headed north on Freeway 5 for a snack lunch at Laguna Beach. We left the freeway at San Clemente to join the PCH, as the Pacific Coast Highway is called, crawling through the never-ending stop light intersections of the coastal resorts. As we were leaving Dana Point for Laguna Beach we set off to cross Ritz-Carlton Boulevard, where our car decided to take control, turning left into the boulevard and left again into the driveway of this swanky hotel. Clearly this was where we were destined to have our snack lunch. The valet parking attendant recommended the lobster tacos served in the ocean front dining lounge under the clear blue sky and where all the waitresses wear sunglasses and identical outfits so it is really hard to remember which one served you. The tacos were small yet tasty and, with our side order of fries and Blue Moon beer, went down a treat.

Having enough of crawling through the main drag of Laguna Beach we took the next right turn heading back to the freeway. We found a toll road over the San Joaquin Hills meeting the 405 at Irvine. The 405, also known as the San Diego Freeway, was five lanes wide with every lane ignoring the speed limit and cruising at 75mph, which was scary enough, but they are all on the wrong side of the road too! Lane discipline is a non-concept over there, with cars and motorcycles overtaking on the inside as well as the outside lanes – but craziest of all was this motorcyclist ahead of us who was weaving, at speed, across all five lanes then back again, seemingly playing a deadly 'snaking' game. The traffic started to back off from this lunatic at around the same time I spotted his brown-shirted uniform and shouted, "It's a ChiP!".

"What's that?" asked Susie, who clearly did not watch the 1970s American television series about the California Highway Patrol, with Officers 'Ponch' Poncherello and Jon Baker. With great skill, and no less courage, our ChiP slowed all five lanes of traffic to a halt and, after parking his bike in the middle of the freeway, calmly walked to remove sizeable chunks of lorry tyre debris that would have been a serious hazard to the high speed traffic. I later discovered that this manoeuvre is the standard technique for controlling traffic flow and would, I imagine, require a lot of practice to perfect.

Back on our way, we joined the Ventura Freeway 101 to the turn-off for Ojai, where we had an overnight stay with Susie's brother Bill and his girlfriend, who is also called Susie. The girls were not entirely comfortable with brother Bill's straightforward way of distinguishing one from the other, the sobriquets of 'Older Susie' for his elder sister and 'Younger Susie' for his girlfriend, although, in fairness, Younger Susie seemed somewhat happier with her new name. We enjoyed a delicious Mexican meal in one of the local restaurants with the siblings catching up on family and friends news.

The Electric Spark that Jumps

Bill was proud to show us his renovated Essex car. It was originally built in 1933 by the Hudson Motor Car Company of Detroit and christened a 'Terraplane' after Amelia Earhart was reputed to have said that driving the car was, to her, the closest land sensation to flying a plane. Bill had owned a Terraplane in his youth and, some fifty years later, regretted selling it way back when. His elder brother, Johnnie, spotted a dilapidated Terraplane for sale that Bill might like to restore. It was not the straight eight-cylinder version noted for its high speed and favoured by 1930's gangsters (notably John Dillinger and Baby Face Nelson and latterly by Hartville's notorious younger sibling of Susie, 'Billy Boy' Brothers). Now, after a few years of loving restoration, the V6 Terraplane rides again.

After breakfast on the patio, shared with the hummingbirds, we set off to the Santa Ynez Valley to enjoy an overnight stop in the Marriott Hotel, where I spent, in one big blowout, all of my accumulated Marriott loyalty points to enjoy a hotel bill that came to a big fat zero dollar total. Whoopee!

Nearby is the town of Solvang, which was settled by Danish immigrants and built in the architecture style of the Denmark they had left behind. It is interesting, different, and fun, but has an unmissable theme park flavour, with windmills, a Copenhagen Square, and a King Frederik Inn. It does have one outstanding restaurant, however, the Root 246, attached to Hotel

Corque. It was not only the comfort level of rediscovering tasteful European decor in the restaurant, it was also the pleasure of a short and straightforward menu which delivered well-cooked food where the flavours of the meal surpassed the marketing hype of the menu description. A rare find indeed.

San Simeon was a couple of hours' drive north, which we travelled in meandering style, stopping off at the little town of Harmony to visit its cafe and eighteen inhabitants. The area was settled by Swiss immigrants in the late nineteenth century, around several dairy ranches. Rivalries between the ranchers led to a killing and, in 1907, the feuding was called off and the settlement renamed Harmony to reflect the new spirit between the farmers and residents. Today there is a craft community with a glassworks, wine maker, and candle maker stores supported by the one small cafe, in a wooden shed complete with turntable and LPs from the 1940s and 50s, ably run by chef Guiseppe. He makes good Italian coffee as well as delicious pastries.

I had booked for us to stay two nights at the Madonna Inn in San Luis Obispo. The Madonna family, no relation to her of the singing voice and conical boobs, were also Swiss immigrants, who made good in construction and cattle ranching before branching into the tourist business. A second visit to this gaudy and iconic hotel was a must. This time I chose the 'Rock Bottom' room which, as the name indicates, is a subterranean cave, beyond the ken of Fred and Wilma Flintstone. Did they enjoy a kingsize double bed or stained glass windows with cherubic and heart-shaped motifs or a rock cave shower room with two shower heads, one sprinkle hose and one monsoon style? Was their hand basin made from a large clam shell with pink and white flower light bulb holders above the oval gilt mirror? I think not, but we did and ours was!

San Simeon, a short drive north, was the location for Hearst Castle, the home of the newspaper magnate and ridiculously wealthy William Randolph Hearst. Construction started in 1919 and was still continuing in 1947 when ill health paused the never-ending project. Its 250,000 acre site, its buildings, and fourteen miles of coastline (ownership of which was only one part of the Hearst property portfolio) now belongs to California and is a state historic park. The architecture is a myriad of styles, as took Hearst's fancy on his world travels, with a preponderance of Southern Spanish influence among the Renaissance and Baroque styles mixed with

South American and Californian influences. The pace of building never seemed to keep up with Hearst's purchases of European art objects or exotic animals for his private zoo in the grounds.

The opulence is overwhelming and the extravagance is unbelievable. Does one really need a pergola of over a mile in length through which one rode on horseback? Or, indeed, an outdoor Neptune Pool with a facade of a Roman Temple as well as a palatial indoor Roman Pool decorated from floor to ceiling with mosaic tiles of intense blue and orange colours suffused with gold? Not to mention the Greek and Roman marble statues that seem to be everywhere. But the visual experience is breath-taking and its location unquestionably spectacular. Worth a visit? Definitely, although a viewing of the Orson Welles portrayal of William Hearst and the mansion in Citizen Kane is worthwhile preparation for the occasion.

It was a risk that viewing the elephant seals on the beach at Piedras Blancas might have been a disappointment after Hearst Castle, but not a bit of it. Hundreds of fat blubbery females and their chubby pups lazing on the beach and rocks sunning themselves, with occasional barking, stretches, or using their flippers to shovel showers of sand over their recumbent bodies, made an irresistibly pleasurable sight until we both agreed we probably had enough photos by now.

The Electric Spark that Jumps

The plan for my third visit to San Luis Obispo was by air. I had renewed my friendship with Adam Messier, who now has moved from full to part-time instructing at Pinnacle Aviation in order to pursue a growing business opportunity as a charter pilot for wealthy Californians who can choose the luxury of personalised air travel without having to remove their shoes, belts, and empty their pockets in the demeaning security searches that are now sadly necessary yet universally tedious and time consuming with commercial flights. Good luck, Adam, with your new business, and may you soon grow your fleet of aircraft from the one twin-propeller Seneca to a fleet of Gulfstream jets.

Adam had big news. His wife, Maurissa, was expecting their first child in June. They already knew it was a boy and had chosen the name 'Fletcher'. Strong name, with images of a young Marlon Brando playing Fletcher Christian as he challenges Captain Bligh's harsh authority on HMS Bounty. The choice of a second name is still a work in progress.

For our first flight on Tuesday we took a Cessna 172, known to her friends as Seven Sierra Papa, to the Mojave Desert. Our intention had been to land at Mojave Airfield, but pilot reports gleaned en-route forecast very turbulent landing conditions. After a brief cockpit discussion we diverted to another airfield in the desert, this one being Victorville. The landing was still lively among the restless thermals from the hot desert sands but I managed a smooth touch down. The fixed base operator for incoming private flights was the delightfully named Million Air facility. The smiling receptionist said we had no need to pay a landing fee (now there is a girl who knows the way to a pilot's heart) and furthermore presented us with Million Air token bank notes entitling us to a $1 lunch. I decided to treat Adam to lunch today!

We booked our aircraft for a second flight on Friday, this time for a flight north along the Pacific coastline to San Luis Obispo. Our route would take us into the busy airspace of Los Angeles International Airport. We could choose one of the four prescribed visual routes and it was a no-brainer for me to opt for the low-level routing over the top of the LAX runways. Low level meant 2,500 feet above sea level and some accurate flying to stick to the narrow corridor that was our permitted bit of the sky today. We took off from McClellan-Palomar Airfield minutes after an historic Mustang fighter aircraft had landed. The Mustang was the vanguard for three restored World War II aircraft due to visit for the weekend. Arriving later that afternoon would be a B17, the famous Flying Fortress, and a B24 Liberator. We hoped to be able to see them on our return.

We had one uncertainty for the day's flight, which was the fires raging out of control in Ventura County to the north of LA. The aviation authorities had put a temporary flight restriction zone around the heart

The Electric Spark that Jumps

of the fire to allow the water bombers to attack the fires without having to worry about looking out for other transiting aircraft. We could route around the TFR but had to be aware of changing wind patterns moving the thick smoke into our planned aerial pathway.

We left the coastline at Long Beach, flying overhead the Queen Mary liner, now a luxury floating hotel, to request clearance to enter LAX airspace for the mini route crossing at two thousand five hundred feet over the city of Los Angeles. Looking across the starboard wing we could see Los Alamitos Military Airfield and the public airfield of Long Beach, with Zamperini Airfield off our left wing. As we crossed overhead the centre line of the parallel east-west runways, we were

excited to see a commercial jet land underneath us. We had a great view of the airliners parked at the terminal gates awaiting passengers for their international journeys.

Our routing continued to Santa Monica Airfield, tracking the SMO radio beacon, after which we received clearance to climb. And climb we needed to, as we could now see the smoke from the fires ahead of us. We judged that we would be above the smoke at 6,500 feet but were mistaken; we found ourselves closing on a thick dark grey cloud and could smell the fumes from the fire permeating our cockpit air.

We headed further east, where the sky was lighter, and climbed further to 8,500 feet. By now, we were getting tossed about by the rising heat from the fires and I was kept busy maintaining the aircraft in a level flying attitude, but we were, at last, above the thickest dark grey smoke clouds. Being aware that later this afternoon we had to fly back through this smoke hazard with no predictability of its location or the then fury of the fires, we began to rethink our destination plans. Perhaps San Luis Obispo was an airfield too far today, so we tapped Santa Barbara into our GPS for a new compass heading and decided we would review things from there.

"Follow Highway 101 north along the coast and report left base leg for runway one five," were the instructions from the Santa Barbara approach controller. This was a bit surprising, as the wind was from 230 degrees, giving us a landing with eighty degrees of crosswind! Even more surprising as there was a second runway pretty much directly into the wind. Our request for a straight in approach for runway two five was politely declined, so I got the opportunity for some more crosswind landing practice. Weathercocking the plane sideways on finals, I kicked her straight with lots of left rudder when we were ten feet off the ground, while simultaneously using the cross control technique of putting the ailerons into a hard right turn to counteract the wind, trying to flip the aircraft over onto its side. We made it!

Over lunch, we discussed how we would get home. Although San Luis Obispo was only ninety miles to the north, this trip was shelved for another day. For now we were focused on how to get round the Ventura County fires for our journey back to base. Going south east to get further inland had the disadvantage of putting us over the mountains, with the possibly of poor visibility, while the coastal route was beset with restricted zones, military areas, and controlled airspace. The coastal route won our vote, and we set off for home at 1500 feet over the water to see if we could get underneath the smoke plumes, whilst keeping a couple of alternative back-tracking routes up our sleeves if coastline proved to be a 'no go'.

As we approached Ventura County and moved five miles out to sea to stay clear of the TFR zone, we could see the seat of the fires clearly, with the big, thick column of smoke rising high into the sky and a mushroom-shaped cloud spreading in all directions. The good news was that we had plenty of clear air below the canopy of this smoky tree for us to fly underneath. As we passed the writhing column of smoke, with red flames flickering on the ground, we saw three 'water' bomber aircraft flying into the dense smoke, followed by an orange carpet of fire retardant falling like a blanket over the scorched ground. Los Angeles cleared us through their airspace once more, this time southbound, and two hours after leaving Santa Barbara we touched down on the McClellan-Palomar westerly runway, with the B17 and B24 waiting for us alongside our parking spot.

The Electric Spark that Jumps

And that is why I didn't get to San Luis Obispo for the third time – at least not this year.

Tusen Takk

Norway 6 to 14 July 2013

G-BOPA
Derek Alway
Paul Edwards

G-IJAG
Robin Wicks
Lety Wicks

Tusen Takk

We were on our way home from Norway, approaching the Bovingdon beacon at 2,300 feet with just eleven miles to go to the Denham Airfield, when the engine suddenly stopped. Paul, who was in the P1 seat, immediately depressed the carb heat control to clear any ice that might be in the carburettor, only to find that there was no problem there. I was in the P2 seat, with navigation and radio responsibilities, and recalled a similar incident a few years back, when I was in the P1 seat returning to Denham from a flight north to play golf on the Royal Birkdale course in Lancashire with Deryck Sutton.

"Change tanks," I called to Paul over the intercom, as I reached forward and flicked the fuel pump switch to the 'ON' position.

Paul reacted at once and changed the fuel control lever from the right tank to the left tank. The propeller was still windmilling as we glided earthwards, and as the fuel was pumped back into the empty carburettor and sprayed into the hungry cylinders we heard the engine restart, the spark plugs igniting the explosive petrol and air mixture. It was a reassuring sound, and we had hardly lost three hundred feet in altitude.

Checking the fuel gauges, we found the right tank empty, with the left tank a third full. We had dutifully switched between the left and right tanks every half an hour of our three hour flight, but somewhere along the way the messages to the fuel tanks had become corrupted. But that is why we practise emergency procedures with regularity so that we can remain calm, think clearly, and solve the problem. If all else fails then we glide the aircraft, at 80 knots, to a landing in a nearby field – and we practise that too!

This was our return flight from a flying tour of Southern Norway. For some reason, Norway had escaped a flying visit during BOPA's European travels. We had visited Sweden, Denmark, and Finland, including a hop across the Baltic Sea to Tallinn in Estonia. We had flown south through France to Italy, Spain, and Portugal. Our log books record our trips east to Poland, Hungary, Czech Republic, Latvia, and Croatia, but not Norway. This year, 2013, was the time to remedy the situation.

Paul Edwards and I crewed G-BOPA, and our friends Robin and his wife Lety, in G-IJAG, made up the two plane squadron for this adventure. With the Saturday showing sunny weather and clear skies, Paul and I

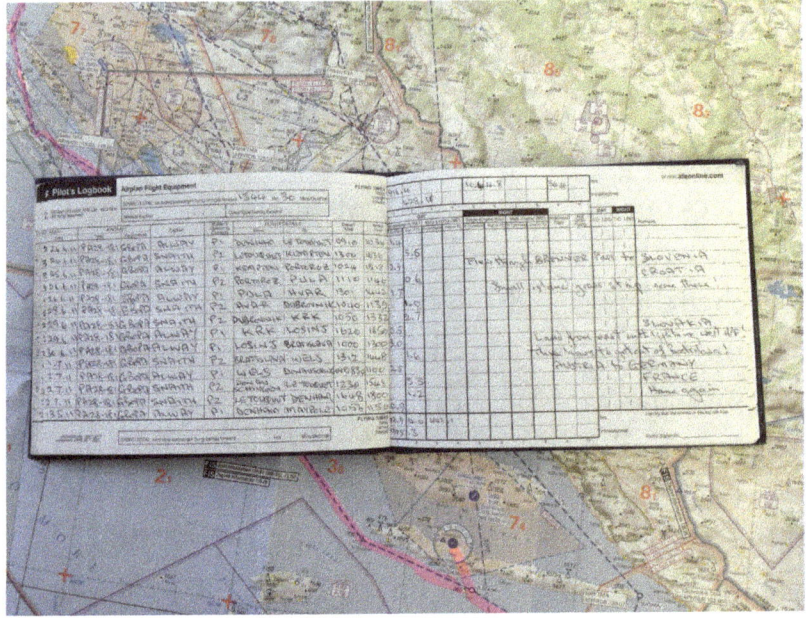

jumped the gun and left a day earlier than planned so that we could sneak in a landing and overnight stop on the German island of Helgoland. This used to be called Heligoland when I collected stamps, although I was not around when Britain swapped the island for Zanzibar with the Germans in 1890! The island is small, actually very small, at one square kilometre for the 'Big' island, while a smaller sister island, Dune, is just over half as big. The airfield is on Dune, with its longest runway at 480 metres, which does not leave too much island until one reaches the water on the far side. We brought BOPA in low and slow over the beach, causing a few holiday makers to duck, and put her landing gear firmly on the tarmac at the start of the 33 northerly runway.

"Zee taxi leaves in ten minutes," said the German accent, and we climbed aboard for the short ride to the dock.

With true German efficiency, the taxi linked with the ferry boat for the half mile ride across the bay to the main island. As we docked, the public address speakers on the boat delighted us with a patriotic song about Helgoland performed by what sounded like the male voice choir and accordion band of the Sixth Panzer Division of Schleswig Holstein. Stirring stuff – and a great welcome. The main island, which has a pedestrian-only policy save for the fire engine and ambulance, is very rocky and in three parts. Unterland at sea level, where our hotel was, the almost two hundred feet higher Oberland where we ate dinner, and Mittelland, created

The Electric Spark that Jumps

by the British Royal Navy when they tried, unsuccessfully, to blow up the island after the war! At least they set the record for the largest conventional weapons explosion – but which Navy Brass thought you could blow the top off a huge undersea mountain? Good to know our taxes are spent wisely.

Sunday morning remained sunny with clear skies as we made our short field take off for Sylt, one of the North Frisian Islands. Sylt is a long thin island buzzing with cars, as well as bus services, even a railway line. The southern half of the island is about six miles off the coast of Northern Germany and the northern half is off the coast of the Danish Jutland peninsula. We checked into the Sylter Hof hotel around midday and were joined shortly afterwards by Robin and Lety, who had left Denham earlier that morning, stopping once at Calais to clear customs into the European Schengen area.

Sylt is a chic holiday resort, with lovely hotels, restaurants, and beaches that are entered only through a manned gate, where one shows your hotel passcode or pays a fee. The beach area is immaculate, litter-free with up-market beach stalls that would not look out of place in St. Tropez or Monte Carlo. Lety was taken by the Sylt sun loungers (as modelled by Lety and Paul), which are made of wicker with an adjustable canopy, upholstered seating, leg rests, and fold-out drinks trays. This was five star  relaxation, and I suspect there might be delivery of one of the two-seater models, with yellow and white striped cushions, to Gerrards Cross in the near future.

After lunch and a walk on the beach, Paul and I went to the Sonntagkonzerte in the local church of St. Nicolai to hear an organ recital. The church has two organs, and the first half of the concert was played by Christian Otto on the larger Kemper pipe organ at the rear of the nave. For the second half, Christian came downstairs to the smaller, brighter-sounding and compact Neuthor pipe organ, situated behind the pulpit. Bach featured, with his thunderous chords, as well as the varied styles and lighter pieces of Reger, Reda, Stanley, and Zachow.

Our evening meal was at the Schnekenhaus restaurant which, as the name suggests, served a starter dish of

The Electric Spark that Jumps

delicious garlicky snails. Delightful restaurant, excellent meal, and friendly service.

So now it was time for the main event. Fly to Norway.

We set off after breakfast, flying over the flat green countryside of Jutland, where the fields seem to merge into the sea. From the north west tip of Denmark, with Aalborg off to our right, we set off across the seventy-mile sea crossing of the Skagerrak for our landing at Kristiansand, on the southern tip of Norway.

Approaching the Norwegian coastline, one cannot help but be entranced by its beauty. There were dozens, no, hundreds if not thousands of islands around the coast, with myriad waterways weaving between them and penetrating deep into the mainland. The islands vary in size from small grey barren rocks smoothed over

by the elements to large green islands bursting with luxuriant vegetation and dotted with colourful timber holiday homes. On that day, the sea was a bright navy blue as we flew to the east of Kristiansand town and across the harbour, for a landing on the south westerly runway 22 of Kjevik Airport.

Steinar was there to meet us: tall, lean, and fit, with his chiselled face, white hair, and beard. He looked very Norwegian, but I guess he would do! He is the cousin of Kari, Angela's friend, who was the librarian in Beaconsfield before retiring. Kari and Steinar grew up together, spending long summer holidays in Kristiansand sailing, crabbing, fishing, and swimming during the long daylight hours.

"My first name means stone," said Steinar, "and my second name, Berge, means mountain, so I am really Rocky Mountain," he continued, with twinkling pale blue eyes behind his large horn-rimmed spectacles. So from then on he was 'Rocky' to me.

After a motorised tour of the old town of Kristiansand, we dropped off our cases at the Radisson Hotel and set off with Steinar for the drive to Trysnes, where our first task was to get ice creams.

"I am now of an age," said Rocky, "when I no longer have to ask if I can have an ice cream – so I have one every day!" I was liking this man more and more.

The five of us climbed into the motorised rowing boat, which Steinar steered across the Trysnes Fjord to the island where he has his holiday cottage. Made of

wood, the grey-boarded, cabin-style cottage faced down the fjord. Grete was on the jetty to meet us and help us ashore for a snack lunch of bread, cheese, and ham, with salad. It was mid-afternoon, and our last meal had been breakfast on Sylt, so we were hungry.

We found it hard to look away from the view across the water over nearby rocks, to the pine forests clinging to the steep sides of the fjord and the colourful wooden cottages peeking out from the trees on the opposite bank.

We lay on sun loungers and all of us succumbed to an afternoon nap in the shade. When we revived, Steinar was ready to take us salt water fishing for mackerel. Donning our borrowed naval hats, we set off on the water, around the islands, and into likely spots where the mackerel might be biting. We trailed the line with its hooks spaced every two feet or so and slowly worked the line, seeking a bite. Steinar got the first bite but, seeing the fish was a sei, pollack, which was declared unsuitable, he threw it back. Shame really, because no matter how we tried that was our only catch of the fishing trip!! Luckily, Grete had been fishing earlier in the day and caught half a dozen mackerel, which were barbecued. Fresh fish off the grill in the open air, smell of sea and pine woods around, and a view to die for; a feast for kings.

I had brought a present for our hosts, a bottle of Highland Park single malt whisky distilled in the

Orkneys. Anxious to avoid embarrassing myself by giving a gift which had deteriorated during its twelve years in the bottle I suggested a precautionary sampling in case I needed to return faulty goods. We were lucky and everyone had a second dram just to make absolutely sure.

We wished Grete farewell and "tusen takk", literally a thousand thanks, for wonderful hospitality. Rocky Mountain took us back to our hotel and, after his thousand thanks were delivered safely, we crashed into our beds.

And another "tusen takk" for Kari, whose introduction to Steinar and Grete led to this wonderfully memorable day.

Our plan had been to fly north to Ålesund, but this was thwarted by a band of rain and cloud stretching north from Stavanger across Bergen and covering Ålesund. As is the way with flying, the weather makes changes to the plan, since there is little point flying in cloud when one is on a sight-seeing flight! So we went to Oslo instead.

The weather-frayed coastline route provided never-ending photo opportunities as we flew over what were unknown Norwegian towns to me: Lillesand, Arendal, Sandefjord, Fredrikstad, and along the length of the finger-shaped Oyeren Lake into Kjeller Airfield, next to the town of Lillestrom at the head of the lake. This was a small airfield, shared with the military, which is much closer to the city of Oslo than the main airport of Gardermoen to the north.

After checking in to our hotel, the concierge directed us to a cheaper and nearby café-cum-bar, where we had a Greek meze snack lunch, along with four large beers. Excellent fare, but the bill came as a surprise when we found that one large beer in Norway costs the equivalent of £15! That's almost five times the cost of a pint of beer at The Green Man pub in Denham Village. We learned that just about everything in Norway is expensive compared to England, and perhaps most European countries too. Best to just bite the bullet, enjoy one's visit, and at least everything will seem really cheap when you get home!

The Electric Spark that Jumps

The Oslo equivalent of London's Oxford Street is Karl Johans Street, which runs from Oslo Central Railway Station to The Royal Palace, passing by Oslo Cathedral, Oslo Museum, and the parliament buildings on the way. By and large it was a disappointing walk that felt grubby, littered, and thronged with begging Romas, hoodies, and Hari Krishna chanters. Not unlike Oxford Street really!

We swung left towards the harbour area and the mood changed to light and airy cleanliness, with an enjoyable coffee stop at Radhusgata in the older part of town. Further on, we were entranced by the Norwegian National Ballet and Opera building with its dramatic stone ski slopes, framing the clean modern architectural lines of the white stone building, which run down to the water's edge. Do the Norwegians ski down these slopes when they're covered in winter snow, stopping just short of plunging into the freezing waters of Bjorvika harbour? We decided that we liked Oslo now.

Dinner that evening was in the Aker Brygge area, where we chose the Onda restaurant, overlooking the yacht-filled marina. An excellent meal outdoors, where a rug is provided on the back of one's chair should it get chilly as the evening goes on. Our waitress was an archetypal Norwegian heroine with freckled fair skin, straw blonde hair, and piercing blue eyes. We were all surprised when she said her name was Asia, and she came from Poznan in Poland! Easy to fool our romantic imaginations.

The skies were clear on the following morning as we planned our flight over the Hardangervidda mountain plateau to Bergen. Our route took us over Vemork, site of the German heavy water plant that was destroyed by Norwegian resistance fighters to sabotage the enemy's atomic weapons programme, which required large volumes of heavy water. And we spotted the hydro-electric dam that provided the power for the heavy water plant, from eight and a half thousand feet, tucked into the end of a long thin lake in one of the many cleaved valleys in these round-topped, snow-capped mountains.

Approaching Bergen, the harsh mountain scenery softens into fractured and rocky coastline, inlets,

harbours, and ubiquitous islands. We advised air traffic of our landing slot authorisations and were directed to enter their airspace by visual reference point, 'Paradis'. So we visited 'Paradise' and returned for a landing on the northerly runway 35 in blustery winds.

Dinner was in the open air again, down in the harbour area, sitting on wooden benches under canvas tenting and savouring creamy fish soup with submerged mussels, and following that with grilled fresh fish and a large plate of crispy chips.

The next day was a no fly day, to give us an opportunity to explore Bergen. The morning was reserved for the visit to Grieg's House in Troldhaugen, as that would allow us to hear the lunchtime piano recital of his music.

The house sits atop the steep rock cliffs of a fiord with views of peace and tranquillity. The house is, unsurprisingly, made of wood, two storeys with a square turret, painted on the outside in cream with bottle green borders and a steeply pitched roof with grey fish-scale tiles. The inside of the house is unpainted to retain the gentle aroma of pine. Although the location is as quiet as a church mouse's footsteps, Grieg was troubled by the hum of the electric lightbulbs, inaudible to anyone else, so had a separate, candle-lit composing cabin erected at the bottom of the garden.

A small concert hall has since been built, with its roof covered in grass turves, kept cropped by goats. The Steinway concert grand sits on a stage which has a large

The Electric Spark that Jumps

window at the back, affording a view that falls away to Nordas Lake below as one looks past the rose bay willow herbs and trees in summer leaf. For our visit, the highly accomplished pianist was Tor Espen Aspaas, who selected various romantic era pieces including Butterfly, excerpts from his piano sonata, symphonic dances and the very moving 'Jeg Elsker Dig' ('I Love You') written for his sweetheart Nina, which he gave as his engagement present to the love of his life.

The afternoon was set aside for our boat ride on the White Lady, along the Osterfjorden. Despite being one of the smaller fiords around Bergen, this still involved four hours of sailing. Extra woollies were needed for the chill of the sea air breeze, as we alternated between sitting outside, wrapped up in the ship's blankets, and retreating to the cabin for a glass of wine and a warm-up. But it was a 'must do' trip to savour the majesty and raw beauty of the sea, the vertical rock cliffs of the fiords, and the remoteness of this part of the world. We enjoyed the scenery in July sunshine but it must be a harsh and challenging place during the dark winter days.

Once again the weather gods decided the route of our travels. Low cloud moved in along the north west coast of Norway and was forecast to remain there for at least three days. We could get above the cloud to fly north but we would either be unable to land when we got to our destination or, if there was a break in clouds for landing then, we risked being stuck there for three or more days.

The new plan involved flying south to Aarhus in Denmark, where we spent a pleasant evening in this university town and had one of the best tenderloin steaks ever. This was the farewell dinner for Robin and Lety who were returning to Denham the next day, to allow Robin time to prepare for his business trip to Monrovia, the capital city of Liberia, in a couple of days.

We left together after breakfast on Saturday morning and flew above the clouds to a lunchtime stop at Bremerhaven in Germany. On recommendation from the radio operator in the tower, we walked half a mile down the road and enjoyed a bratwurst and chips lunch at the yacht club.

We waved goodbye to Robin and Lety as they departed for home, then Paul and I flew to another Frisian island, this time off the coast of Holland. This holiday island is called Texel but pronounced 'Tessel' in Dutch – not that either of us spoke any Dutch! The welcome at the airfield was most cordial, as I received a big smile, warm handshake, and a "Welkom" from Mike in the tower. I had now doubled my Dutch vocabulary! Mike asked where we were staying and, on being told it was the Tesselhof Hotel, he said that his father, Ed, would be happy to give us a lift to the De Koog beach resort where our hotel was located. Ed and

Mike own and run the Texel Airfield with efficiency and an approach to customer service that makes you start planning your return visit before you have left.

Ed recommended the Orangerie restaurant for our evening meal and it turned out to be a good choice. Despite learning my third Dutch word, 'kip', for chicken, I chose the local lamb for main course after a starter of Grandma's recipe soup which had bits of 'kip' in it.

I guess we were both tired as neither Paul or I were kept awake by the revellers at the all night beach party. This probably explains the lack of young people at breakfast the next morning.

Paul and I took a walk to the beach, inspecting the shoreline to see if the wet sand would support a landing in an emergency. We decided it would and to keep as close to the water's edge as possible!

The flight home was straightforward. We chose to fly along the Dutch coast at below 1500 feet to remain underneath the Amsterdam and Rotterdam control zones. Once clear, we climbed to 4000 feet over the top of Ostend before setting out across the English Channel for Manston on the Kent coast. We landed at Denham just before one o'clock, completed the aircraft technical log and put BOPA to bed with a pat and a 'Tusen Takk' for another flying adventure together.

The Electric Spark that Jumps

Naked Virgins Dancing on the Village Green

It was Simon's idea to participate in the pagan rituals to celebrate the first day of summer, despite the distinct possibility of finding ourselves selected to sit on the reserves bench for the fertility rites. The only snag, as far as I could see, was that with festivities commencing at dawn on the first day of May, an early start was required for us to be in place for the 5.32am sunrise. Mark you, it's a good thing that summer doesn't start on the first of June, since the sun is scheduled to rise at 4.49am that day.

The event was being held in the car park of The Royal Standard of England pub in Forty Green. Simon decided to walk to the pub with his dogs: two black Labradors and two border terriers. Whilst this had the benefit of giving the dogs an early morning chase through Hogback Woods, it did have the downside of a start to the day at shortly after four-thirty. Using the benefits of wisdom that comes with time, I'd opted to drive, allowing me a further fifteen minutes of sleep.

We arrived in good time before festivities commenced and were delighted to find the pub open and serving coffee, although Simon could not resist

the rare opportunity for a glass of ale to start the day. Wandering back out of the pub into the car park, we mingled with jingling Morris Men and maidens of indeterminate ages, lacking any obviously virginal glow or indeed promise of tantalising glimpses of their female delights.

In front of the assembled early risers, eight Morris dancers from the Grand Union troupe, or more correctly a 'Side', formed up and gave forth with a vocal greeting to the dawn. The waistcoated and top-hatted squeeze-box players led them into their traditional hopping dance. This Cotswold Side was dressed in white breeches and loose-fitting shirts banded with crossed braids on the fronts and backs of their chests. Bell-pads were buckled below the knees and their black hats were highly decorated with flowers, badges and ribbons. The chest braids, or baldrics, were yellow and black striped, mimicking the costume colours for The Fool – who, as the title might suggest, was of little or no help to the dancers.

Thinking that was it for the morning, we started to anticipate breakfast when twelve maidens, not quite in the springtime of their youth, formed up in front of us in costumes that would not have been out of place in a puritanical village scene of the 17th century. These were the 'Flowers of May' dancers from Harrow, wearing dresses of cornflower blue and red pinafores with long white kerchiefs hanging from their waists, completing the outfits with black clogs, small blue headscarves and beribboned batons. Their music was provided by a man playing an accordion supported by two fiddle players and percussion. The ladies had great fun and were very nimble on their feet, their sheer enjoyment of the dance well-conveyed to the morning watchers. Good for them.

A passing farmhand on his way to morning milking might have been somewhat surprised and perplexed to see the belly dancers forming up as if from a scene in Arabian Nights. Were these the naked virgins? Almost certainly not, but at least we were treated to eight bare bellies writhing and pulsating to the sound of Middle Eastern music played on a snake charmer's pipe and North African drums mixing with the women's

ululating tongues. Such exotic costumes, in bright colours with long flowing skirts and bra-tops highly decorated with frills, lace, bangles and beads framing the exposed midriffs, which sported occasional tattoo designs and bellybutton rings of gold. An ethnic treat of gyrating tummies, wiggling hips and flowing hand movements, which had a definite hint of come hither and beguiled us all.

And so it was, repeating this sequence, that the three troupes treated us to two more dances each in turn. The men enjoyed crossing their strong thick sticks, each one seeking to outdo the others with the force of the strike whilst avoiding bruising their own knuckles. The maturing maidens of Harrow wove patterns with their kerchiefs and the Belly Dancers balanced shining

scimitars on their heads whilst spinning around to the sounds of a melancholy tribal wail.

The pub landlord, Matthew, dressed unsoberly in purple cord trousers and pink shirt, had organised for his chef to provide us all with a full English breakfast, served in an instant, and a bottomless coffee pot to hand. What a fabulous way to start the summer. The morning was warm, the sun rose brightly and it was good to be alive and proudly celebrate our English heritage. Shame about the virgins though. I guess they must have been held up somewhere. They would have enjoyed the event so much.

www.ingramcontent.com/pod-product-compliance
Lightning Source LLC
Chambersburg PA
CBHW060044230426
43661CB00004B/651